W9-DCF-674

MEDITATIONS

MEDITATIONS

by

TOYOHIKO KAGAWA

Translated by
JIRO TAKENAKA

GREENWOOD PRESS, PUBLISHERS
WESTPORT, CONNECTICUT

Library of Congress Cataloging in Publication Data

Kagawa, Toyohiko, 1888-1960.
  Meditations.

    Reprint of the ed. published by Harper,
New York.
    1. Meditations.   I.   Title.
BV4839.J3K3   1978   242   78-12761
ISBN 0-313-21180-9

BV
4839
.J3
K3
1979

Reprinted with the permission of Harper & Row, Publishers, Inc.

Reprinted in 1979 by Greenwood Press, Inc.,
51 Riverside Avenue, Westport, CT 06880

Printed in the United States of America

10 9 8 7 6 5 4 3 2 1

Contents

MEDITATIONS

1

THE WELLSPRING OF MEDITATION

SINCE I learned how to enter the forest of meditation, I have received sweet dewlike drops from that forest. I have found that the door to meditation is open everywhere and any time, at midnight or at noonday, at dawn or at dusk. Everywhere, on the street, on the trolley, on the train, in the waiting room, or in the prison cell, I am given a resting place of meditation, wherein I can meditate to my heart's content on the Almighty God who abides in my heart.

It is said that Francis of Assisi meditated and prayed, looking up at the sun in broad daylight. Plato has told how Socrates suddenly would pause and stand erect to meditate for a few minutes while walking with his disciples. According to the Sutra of Agon, Buddha practiced a similar custom. Jesus withdrew into the wilderness and meditated for forty days and forty nights. Sometimes he was lost in meditation and prayer all night long in the mountains of Galilee. Those who draw water from the wellspring of meditation know that God dwells close to their hearts. For those who wish to discover the quietude of old amid the hustle and bustle of today's machine civilization, there is no way save to rediscover this ancient realm of meditation. Since the loss of my eyesight I have been as delighted as if I had found a new wellspring by having arrived at this sacred precinct.

(JOSHUA 1:9)

2

SUFFERING AND FAITH

NOTWITHSTANDING that an Almighty God is defending us from His heavenly throne, we seem beset with hardship and sorrow in this human world. Why has God created pain? Why are there tears as well as smiles on everyone's cheek? Pain, sorrow and grief, all these are whips whereby God stimulates and enlivens us. A whip makes the horse run. Iron becomes steel when it is heated white hot and shines when it is thrust into water and beaten on an anvil. God pushes us into the depths of sorrow with the intention to train and to develop us. No afflictions have ever defeated those who have never lost sight of God. The apostles and saints grew strong and the fiber of their character developed with each new hardship.

The Japanese nation must not flinch before the earthquake disasters it is called upon to bear. We should grow through such testings. God is encouraging the Japanese people through what seems like discouragement.

Through all these trials from God, we must not be overpowered by a temptation to yield. We must grasp the absolute faith of Job who cried, "The Lord gave, and the Lord hath taken away; blessed be the name of the Lord." It is the secret of genuine faith to comprehend after thinking it through that sickness, pain, death and sorrow—everything— are but devices of our Heavenly Father to keep us from being spoiled.

(JOB 1:21)

3

A NEW DISCOVERY

WHAT is meant by an eternal nature being in Jesus?

The meaning is one of "salvation" or "redemption" from God's standpoint, and of "rebirth" from man's standpoint.

Whether there was a possibility of rebirth for man had long been a question until the coming of Jesus. Job's anguish had its source at this point. Job was distressed because "willows have rebirth but man has none."

Jesus answered the question very clearly. It was his unique discovery on the meaning of life. His disclosure was that in God's universe the weak and lonely can ascend and surpass themselves through the aid of God's power. Christ was the discoverer of this eternal principle.

Modern men make light of salvation. As a result, there occur such tragedies as murder and suicide in order to escape from the pressure of ordinary living. In any crisis, however, God's power can be added to ours. There exists a fair land prepared for the downtrodden, the forsaken and the abandoned, where an almighty power offers an opportunity for a new life. The faith that those who are with God always overcome the world is salvation itself and redemption, and the rebirth that Jesus foretold.

(I JOHN 5:4)

4

A FEARLESS RELIGIOUS LIFE

IN a period of the Mediterranean civilization that might be called a period of moral madness, a laborer named Jesus, a carpenter's son, seeing the corruption of society on all sides, began to preach that those conditions could not endure and that true civilization could not come to pass without the intervention of God's power.

The world would not improve without man's love for man, even though one's fellow man be an enemy. This was the starting point of Christianity. Many listeners misunderstood this preacher of love who declared that God is not to be feared but is the Father in heaven.

I lived in lonesome fright up to the age of eleven, in the country of Awa Province. There I was told that we would be cursed for such an act as spitting on the soil, that evil spirits inhabiting mountains, rivers and deep wells would damn us for slight misdeeds. There were supposed to be devils in ponds, water imps in streams, and ghosts in solitary places. Thus I spent my boyhood in the midst of fear and terror. Nowhere in the universe was there love or affection, nor any friend that would sustain me. It was the greatest joy for me to learn finally that the essence of the universe is love and that God is a merciful Father.

The good tidings of Jesus lie in the belief that the essence of the universe is an affectionate Creator, however dark the night may be and however fiercely the tempest may roar. Here is the infallible remedy for moral madness. And this is the power of Christianity that has completely refashioned one-third of this world's history.

(I JOHN 4:18)

5

CHALLENGE OF MATERIALISM

VIRILITY always goes with an adventurous spirit. So-called good men are often too weak to be really virtuous. The biography of such an adventurous humanitarian as Livingstone inspires us. But genuine adventure does not necessarily imply a geographical escapade like the exploration of the dark continent of Africa. What adventure does require always is the spirit to put heart and soul into the quest and the service of the good.

There exist so many internal and external obstacles which hinder us from attaining the virility demanded by this. Even when we have overcome external obstacles, it is truly tragic that our own imperfection hinders us from high adventuring.

We must constantly fight against all sorts of materialism that tramples religion under foot and disregards ideals.

Paul says, "If God be with us, who can be against us?"

Paul again says, "We are troubled on every side, yet not distressed; we are perplexed, but not in despair; cast down, but not destroyed."

No age has ever seen such pressing necessity for fighting materialism as ours. And no struggle has ever needed such boldness and virility as are imperative today. This fight is really a great adventure which demands our utmost of intelligence and perseverance.

(LUKE 9:62)

6

VIRILE SPIRIT

To believe in Christ is to grasp the secret by which we are made virile. Through that faith we never die, even though we appear to do so, and we are never defeated. It is a religious quality of a virile spirit never to despair in the final day of reckoning and to experience even in death the miracle of resurrection. Christ rose from the dead, breaking open the tomb.

How great an undertaking we are committed to! Never fear! In the thick of hardships or of desperation God is with us and watches over us. Fear of the world is nothing to those who have broken out of the grave. We must rise gallantly for the fulfillment of the mission consigned to us by God. About the middle of the first century, when the facilities for traveling were extremely meager, Paul traveled quite alone, sometimes sailing over the Mediterranean Sea where wind and tempest raged, other times plodding afoot from town to town through Asia Minor and Greece, bearing witness to the gospel of Christ.

Lost in admiration, I contemplate the virile figure of Paul. Even one village will suffice for us to do likewise. We can elevate it toward God with this spirit of Paul's. We can create a new epoch wherein all Japan will be infused with the spirit of Jesus. His religion has a dynamic in it. It is love! Love is the final mover.

(I Corinthians 16:13)

7

LOVE IS STRONGER THAN DEATH

ALL kinds of sufferings I have undergone, but no suffering has served as a reason for my denial of love. "Love" working within me is more than able to conquer those sufferings. I do not deny the eventuality of death. Death lies sternly upon my course. Nevertheless, I believe that love has far greater power than death. Death is to be swallowed up into love. Love is stronger than death. Love's glory tramples even death underfoot. I even think that death is transformed through love into an order of art. Death is an aspect of change. But love is the substance that persists through all change. All things under the sun die for love's sake, but rise again for love's sake, too. I know no reason why we should be afraid of death if it fits into love's scheme. I know well the hardships of age and infirmity, but love is able to surpass even these.

Love is perpetual rejuvenation. Even if I am a man who is worn out with years, love, which continually advances ahead of me, provides a wider road. Since I know this, I never will lose my way or be put to confusion.

(I JOHN 3:14-16)

8

A FOOLISH CHRISTIAN!

A FOOLISH Christian! The laughingstock of the world! Yes, indeed, such am I. I have spent half my lifespan as a foolish Christian. All sorts of so-called worldly pleasures have slipped away from me. Never could I enjoy the leisure of a movie. I have spent half my life in a state describable as being tied to a garbage can. Despised as a narrow-minded man, and looked down upon as a stubborn man, I have spent much of each day for half a lifetime in tears.

When I was forced to take my stand at the foot of the Cross, summoned out of a lewd environment, I was labeled a hypocrite, a member of a gang of traitors and heathens. Even among my fellow Christians I am not always welcome. Often I am excluded as a heretic, a socialist, a flippant man, destitute of profound thoughts.

However, all that does not matter in the least. I am a captive of Christ. I am a slave of the Cross. I belong among the foolish. In other words, I have just taken off on a journey to the Holy Mountains, stark naked, throwing all earthly things away. If it appears foolish to the eyes of other people, I can't help it.

(I CORINTHIANS 1:17-19)

9

WANDERING

HAVING no permanent home of his own, spurned by his fellow countrymen, Jesus was like a stranger in an alien land.

He sighed and said, "The foxes have holes, and the birds of the air have nests; but the Son of man hath not where to lay his head."

Indeed, from ancient times, all men who have steadfastly sought after truth have been persecuted by their fellows and have had no native land they could ever call their own. This was the case with Confucius, Mahomet, Buddha, and St. Francis.

Jesus was an extreme example of the rejected. At first he was so popular that he had to flee to the sea or into the mountains to avoid the multitudes, but the moment it became clear to the people that he was not going to start the political revolution the entire Jewish nation expected, and proposed instead making a spiritual revolution, his popularity waned and declined. Soon he became unable to find a safe place wherein to lay his body, and finally he was crucified.

Viewing this from another angle, however, we can say that Jesus, who had no permanent home of his own, possessed a place to live in peacefully anywhere upon the earth. True, Jesus had surrendered all his rights of physical ownership. But this renunciation meant that he had won all these things for himself.

(LUKE 9:57-60)

10

THE CROSS IS A PATH

THE Son of man who had not where to lay his head chose the Cross as his abiding place at the end of a long wandering career. The Cross was the final resting place for the Son of man whose life had little rest in it. Those roamings of his, full of persecution, ill-treatment and suffering, were themselves a foretaste of the Cross. The Cross of Jesus was not wholly contained within the three hours on Calvary. The path the hungry and weary Son of man trod for three years and a half was a long journey along Via Dolorosa. The Via Dolorosa, meaning a sad path, is a narrow street in the walled city of Jerusalem along which Jesus plod bearing his Cross. Till the present day the street remains as it was then.

This brave wanderer who, in order to save mankind, indicated the way for those to follow who also love humanity, and who chose the Cross instead of a crown, is the ever-flowing inspiration to us proletarians. The Cross is our pathway, too. Nobody can enter eternal life without passing through it. It is mere child's play to refuse the Cross and to wish to wear a crown. The wanderer Jesus who made his crown of thorns instead of gold and jewels knew the true recipe for service and its reward.

(JOHN 19:17-18)

11

NATURE AND RELIGION

BYRON said that he liked nature better than he liked man. But to search this statement for its truth, he liked nature because he first liked himself. Only those who love themselves can love mankind. Furthermore, in order to love mankind truly, one must return to nature. Therefore, to like nature as one likes man, truth to tell, must be the real sentiment of all lovers of nature.

When we are weary of our modern city life, where can we find the best place to escape from its complicated mechanical processes?

In theaters? In movie houses? In centers of night life? No! No! No! Our escape must consist in a retreat to nature. Return to nature! Pitiable are those who have forgotten the way to return to nature.

Jesus often eluded the multitudes and departed into a desert place to rest and meditate. There he could appreciate God's creation, for nature is God's art.

(MARK 6:31-32)

12

THE SPRINGTIME OF LIFE

JESUS rolled away the stone, broke open the tomb, tore the graveclothes from himself. Jesus arose. But, strange though it be, this experience of resurrection is repeated in the history of all human beings. Even the earthworm regenerates itself when head or tail is severed from its body. Just as the nail of a finger grows back after having been cut off, so does the soul. Be the soul ever so wounded and mangled, God will dress the sore spot with His bandage of love. And under His healing influence a new infusion of life accomplishes the process of growth. This is the reason why religion is never contradicted by biology or any other science. If any scientific claim is not consistent with religion, that claim is due to a disregard of, or to ignorance of, those activities that constitute life.

Poor people, laborers, slaves and sinners—all can be born again and changed into the redeemed. Right here is demonstrated the power of true religion. Jesus said, "Marvel not that I said unto thee, Ye must be born again."

(JOHN 3:3-7)

13

READINESS FOR DEPARTURE

JAPANESE people, come to Jesus! Get rid of all complexities that interfere, and be imbued with the way of simple love! Japanese Christians, are you ready to start? Are your suitcases packed lightly enough? Attend to your own before you adjust those of the world. And if you are ready, let us set off on the journey straight along the road Jesus went on.

Christ, our Teacher! Christ, our Healer! Christ, our Redeemer! Pray send us—to factories, to farms, to dirty slums, or to germ-infested sanatoriums! Let us go wherever our missions call. What Jesus taught his disciples at their departure can be applied to our setting off. First of all, we must be lightly clothed. Nothing is so convenient as to be lightly burdened. Freedom from baggage is wealth in all truth. If we were living in old days, we would have to march slowly on, a carriage in the feudal lord's procession with gold-lacquered chest carriers leading the procession. But today we need to carry only a single suitcase. Let us advance with only this equipment.

(LUKE 9:3)

14

PRAYER OF SELF-DEDICATION

O GOD, Our Father! May we start with no unnecessary encumbrances. Our souls burn with unquenchable resentment. We are mindful of what the masses will be if we fail to rise to the occasion. We pray that Thou show us clearly the heart of the Kingdom of God. We do not protest even if our life is destined to lead to the Cross, or the way lead to our losing our lives. We will march in the face of distress or contrary winds.

Teach us how to dispense with unnecessary things. Let us go forward without fear of death in order to fulfill our mission simply, surely and steadily. Reveal to us our station clearly and strengthen us that we may be able to teach and guide by our example all sick persons, lepers, and even devils.

We, Thy disciples, are now departing. Though few of us are death-defying in our own strength, may we dare bravely even among wolves. The world we know is now waiting for us with threats and perils. But let us start with a pledge on nonresistance.

We pray that Thou find us worthy to work through us.

In the name of our Lord. Amen.

(EPHESIANS 3:19)

15

THE KINGDOM-OF-GOD MOVEMENT

THE fundamental principle of Christianity is simple to state. Christ said, The time is fulfilled, and the Kingdom of God is at hand. Christianity is no more and no less than the advent of the Kingdom of God. Some people extract "God" from the Kingdom of God to construct a philosophy upon, while others seize on "Kingdom" to carry out a social movement. The latter choice has resulted in social theories and political parties. Thomas Aquinas, on the other hand, emphasized the idea of God. As that system gradually declined, it became an individualistic religion, in which God was separated from the daily life of mankind.

True Christianity, however, is not an individualistic religion but a superindividualistic one. While it is a social movement, it involves the co-operation between God and men. This point should be made clear.

The idea of the Kingdom of God was not clear even to the disciples. That was why Jesus was finally crucified. Judas Iscariot exchanged the Kingdom of God for a "Kingdom" movement, leaving out "God." Seeing that Jesus would not become a king, Judas betrayed him.

Peter, on the contrary, excluded all but God, and forgot the element of love to which he should have bent his energies. Even in the Bible we find places where the idea of the Kingdom of God is sundered and dim. We must consider the meaning of the Kingdom of God in its totality and clarity.

(MARK 1:15)

16

VICTORY THROUGH FAITH

ONLY if we feel inclined to try with power given afresh by God, will we find that wonderful power springing up within ourselves—such tremendous power as we have never thought possible. Jesus often possessed this supernatural power. He said, "Ye shall not have gone over the cities of Israel, till the Son of man be come." He also said, "You'll see that time will come when I rule over the Kingdom of God and I accomplish great things." It came true, wonderfully true. The new religion thus born gradually conquered Rome and spread to the ends of the earth. Jesus trusted in a power that human beings could not possess in themselves. Whenever this wonderful power shall enter again a man who correctly says of himself, "I'm ignorant. I have no more than high school education," all Japan, nay, the whole world will be overturned, and a great undertaking will be accomplished.

Even the most worthless person is assured of a rebirth once he allies himself with Almighty God. That frail girl Joan of Arc rose at the voice of God speaking through her to a defeated and dismembered France. This sixteen-year-old girl retrieved the resources of a vanquished army. Her country's enemies were beaten when she led the troops. Reinforced by this maiden's faith in God, France was stronger than a million soldiers. God always uses for His ends those who seem weak and without merit in themselves.

(I CORINTHIANS 1:26-28)

17

A LIFE OF THANKSGIVING

WE must have within ourselves a spiritual element of "rejoicing in hope; patient in tribulation; continuing instant in prayer." To be patient in tribulation is the result of encouragement through hope. Many will weep with us who weep, but few will rejoice with us who rejoice. We have a proverb that "a stake which raises its head is driven in," but we must not so act toward other persons. Instead we should push up one man after another. It is true love to let those rise in the world who deserve success.

Work under others. Be content to play a subordinate part. If a storekeeper thinks of humbling himself, he cannot be oppressive or tyrannical. No undertaking can be really successful unless both the boss and his men humble themselves and push up others mutually. There are no complaints from one who is devoting his life wholly to God and burning the continuous lights of faith, charity and hope. He enjoys everything always with cheerful heart. Working together, the whole family is in a holiday mood. We feel happy in any sort of job. It is the true Christian life and the true worship of God to be happy whether we are engaged in trading, in office work, or in laboring.

(ROMANS 12:12)

18

THE FUNDAMENTALS OF SOCIAL RECONSTRUCTION

WHAT I am most convinced of by my tour of the world is that no age has ever seen a more pressing need for world adjustment than the one we live in today. I am not referring, now, only to Europe or America, but to my own country, which needs it above all others.

Suppose that we set about making this adjustment; with what sort of standard or intention should we make it? The answer to this initial question is very simple. I say, make a standard of the Kingdom of God that Jesus taught. To start with the intention of the Kingdom of God is the sole way of adjusting today's mismanaged world.

In the Kingdom of God the ideal of Jesus has already taken a concrete shape. Jesus Christ regarded himself as the King of the Kingdom of God. Among the heathen, men who have many employees, or wield authority, or exert the power of mammon are held in esteem; but in the Kingdom of God it is just the opposite. In this realm those are respected who labor, who are oppressed or despised, or who humble themselves to serve others. Here the proud and haughty are weeded out. Many schemes today are presented as infallible programs for remedying the world's ills. But no promise of social reconstruction is so reliable and thoroughgoing as this.

(LUKE 21:22-26)

19

CHRIST'S SPECIALITY

ONCE the end of the world was said to come to pass by a sudden intervention of supernatural power in natural events! The judgment was to be executed upon the righteous and the wicked alike. We must not laugh at such an idea as this. It communicated the gloomy mood of the day when it was believed, a mood most pronounced in the Gospel of Matthew. Therein lay a difference between Mahomet and Jesus. In the Koran, despair rules at the last and there is no assurance of salvation in it. It is true that the virtuous are promised happiness, but for the wicked only despair is left. On the contrary, Jesus, when he became conscious that he was Christ, tried to save even the souls which were on the verge of despair from the gloomy atmosphere of the world's end. He guaranteed salvation as the Messiah or Christ. Even they who were shut out of Judaism, they who were shunned by all groups of the virtuous or excluded by the Romans, even they would never be rejected in the Kingdom of God. These were good tidings of Jesus. By this bond Jesus linked the Old Testament and the New Testament. He assured the salvation of God to that generation immersed in gloom and agony. What the present age demands is after all nothing but a reaffirmation of the Christ revealed in the Gospels.

(ROMANS 7:25)

20

THE BIRTH OF LOVE

WHEN you are in distress, wait for the spell to pass. You will
see the way to walk as you grow old. Japanese young people
have a tendency to agonize when they are disappointed in
love. Those who are dejected I continually advise to wait,
wait with prayer. If we are absorbed in our own affairs, the
agony arising from them will never cease. Tolstoy spent the
first fifty years of his life for the good of himself alone. His
experiences are reflected in his novels—*Anna Karenina, The
Youth, The Cossacks* and *Resurrection*. What Tolstoy first
noticed only at fifty was that despite all his activity he had
never loved others. Thereupon he cast his selfishness aside
and began to love something outside. Thus he found great
light bursting in his soul.

As to the anguish of disappointed love, healing is sure to
come if we surpass our selfishness and feel like doing something for others. Love evolves gradually. We may enlarge
the affectionate heart, changing disappointed love into one
which encompasses the world. Thus is born a great world-
wide love that dissolves the individualistic passion or
ambition.

(EPHESIANS 2:1-2)

21

NEW MORALITY BASED ON GOD

EVEN in Russia, Lenin said, "It is to stand between the new and the old society that I become a dictator." Jesus advocated the virtue of submission as a recipe for the shift from the old society to the new. He meant that he needed not to work assertively since God works through him.

The principle of absolute nonresistance started with the idea that it is better to mobilize God than to exert oneself; that is to say, it made God's intervention the basis of morality. Just for this reason I advocate nonresisting love. The principle of nonresistance cannot be supported with human power alone. Tolstoy says that God will surely avenge, and without that faith everybody will resist. Since God's power is greater than ours, we leave the issue to God. Those who observe this technique of love, of righteousness, and of submission, are assured of a victory. This is a truth that the history of the past two thousand years validates. The fall of the Roman Empire and the triumph of Christ are examples of this fact.

God saves even sinners. If there were no salvation, nonresistance would be a folly. In the interest of salvation, therefore, we deny violence. This sentiment is expressed in Jesus' Sermon on the Mount.

(MATTHEW 5:39-42)

22

LOVE AND THE NATURE OF GOD

THERE is no revelation but love. God should not be sought for in books, nor in the organization of institutions. God should not be looked for theoretically but God should be loved. God reveals Himself only in love. One who loves to hear the voice of God should love Him. God is understood best where there is abundance of love. Tolstoy says, "Where there is love, there is God." John says too, "He who loves not, knows not God; for God is love."

Love awakens all it touches. Love whispers to the ear and arouses the heart. Love speaks to all people making them understand that creation is only the art of life pursued for love. Creation is an ornament designed by love. Creation itself is a perfect drama—a drama in which love redeems every suffering and every misfortune. For love, everything that exists is a victory. Everything is created and given for love's sake. Love is alpha and omega, the beginning and ending. Love is the true nature of God. The sanctuary of God is love. I know that I can worship God only in love. All the idols and all the temples and cathedrals are nothing but symbols. I worship God only in love. All forms and ceremonies are mere supplements.

(I JOHN 4:8-9)

23

THE RECORDS OF MIRACLES

TRULY in a world where a sparrow shall not fall to the ground without our Father's permission, God is the friend of the oppressed and the Savior of the downtrodden. The weak and the poor need not give up to discouragement on the mere ground of their defeat in the struggle for existence. (Luke 12:6.) In ancient times when he saved the Israelites from the bondage of slavery under Pharaoh of Egypt, Moses started his campaign of emancipation with only prayer and faith. The Hebrews possessed no facilities for war at all—not a horse nor a chariot. Yet, under God's mysterious protection and in the strength of their faith in His great salvation, God led them by day in a pillar of cloud and by night in a pillar of fire, and they wandered and roamed about the wilderness for forty years. The foolishness of God was wiser than the wisdom of men. These impotent Israelites established an independent nation through their reliance upon God's help. The record of this mysterious rescue remains in Exodus, and the record is a record of miracles. Since then the Israelites have fought many wars. Always their conviction has been that the very existence of their race was due not to military prowess, and that their emancipation from the Egyptian bondage was to be entirely attributed to the power of God's miraculous deliverance.

(EXODUS 13:22)

24

CONQUEST BY GOD

DOMINATED by matter, machinery and mammon, human beings scratch and bite one another like so many cogwheels—at home they quarrel over property, and at work, over division of the profits. This is the condition that obtains today. The question is: How long can society keep going with its existence threatened in this way?

The same condition ruled the Mediterranean civilization in the Roman period two thousand years ago. The Romans held sway over the world by military force, then indulged themselves in sensual pleasures with wealth looted from conquered countries.

Not satisfied with the excitement of commonplace enjoyments, men of prestige and power would divide a thousand slaves into two armies of equal numbers and compel them to fight with swords on the boats on the Tiber River which ran through the capital. These slaves fought desperately for their lives under the promise of freedom from bondage if victorious. The people of the upper classes enjoyed watching the spectacle.

Until Christianity had permeated the Empire, the Romans had not the slightest notion that such an act was a sin. It was Christianity that put an end to these gladiatorial combats that were the cruelest game in history. Not by force, nor by a popular rebellion, but by celestial, mysterious power, Christianity finally conquered that great Empire of old, a huge and mighty organization, its opposite in every respect.

(ROMANS 8:31)

25

PESSIMISM AND JESUS

JESUS is regarded by the world at large as the Man of Sorrows. The Cross as the symbol of suffering is supposed to prove his sorrowing nature. A shadow, it is true, always followed Jesus. But this shadow was really cast by the conditions in Judea at that time.

Some thinkers declare that the original religious sentiment is that of pessimism. Eucken of Germany thought that the essence of religion could be found in pessimism, and argued that the denial of the wicked world is the very source of religious endeavor. Thus it is the heart of a religion to give up a superficial and mechanical attitude to living and take up instead a transcendental point of view.

It is true that Jesus cried, "This wicked generation!" observing the wicked government of King Herod and the tyranny of the Roman Emperor. To a casual glance this seems to be like pessimism. But caution must be exercised that it by no means be made identical with the pessimism that Hindu philosophers dwell upon.

The utterance of Jesus, "This wicked generation!" does not imply an utter denial of the world. He cried, "This wicked generation!" lamenting that people were entering its labyrinth not realizing that they could enter the Kingdom of God by taking the other fork of the road. He lamented only that people took a wrong course; he grieved over their error in making the choice.

(JOHN 17:15)

26

MORE THAN THEORIES

THEORIES change from day to day. On the announcement of the theory of relativity, the Newtonian law of gravitation became shaky and unreliable. Similarly, in case of religion, if its truth is sought on the basis of theories, it becomes outworn at every change of theories. True religion, however, must be grasped by intuition. Its temple should be built on the personal experiences of each and every man. Religion should not be sought for externally, nor should it set a standard merely for the external man. God must be experienced within our own selves.

God is life. He has created me, and in fact He keeps me alive now. The essence of life, nay, life itself, is my God. What I mean by life is by no means physical life exclusively, but the true life that has its existence before this kind of theory was ever invented.

This God of life cannot be revealed clearly by demonstrations. Hence, religious literature is obliged to take a form of allegory. If you were to be asked by someone what sort of thing life is, can you prove what it is? You will never be able to accomplish this by theories.

(MALACHI 3:5-6)

27

THE FOOLISHNESS OF GOD AND THE WISDOM OF MEN

WONDERFUL is the Providence of God's mercy. The rich do not always receive God's grace, nor do the learned necessarily inherit the Kingdom of God. The wise, proud of their wisdom, destroy themselves for the sake of their wisdom, and the sagacious, depending on their sagacity, ruin themselves to augment its amount. On the contrary, the crippled, the disinherited and the poor receive the blessings of God. I shed tears of joy when I reflect on this. It is not because of scholars or millionaires that we inherit the Kingdom of God. God has chosen the foolish things of the world to confound the wise, and the base things of the world to overturn the towers of the mighty. Can we accept that this is the way of God's selection, a way which seems contradictory and paradoxical to us? What do you answer to this?

The art of Pericles' age, Socrates' wisdom, Plato's philosophy, Aristotle's science, the master dramas of Sophocles, Euripides and Aeschylus—such culture Greek civilization possessed; it far surpassed that of Judea. To a tiny branch of that inferior people, David belonged. Generations later, when his pedigree had become uncertain, the son of a carpenter, Joseph, who called himself a descendant of David, was enshrined as the Saviour of the world. By this turn of events, Paul was deeply perplexed. He marveled at the strangeness of God's Providence.

(I CORINTHIANS 1:25)

28

JESUS' SECRECY

JESUS kept secret the fact of his being Christ until the very end of his career. I call it "Jesus' secrecy." Even when Peter said, "Thou art the Christ," Jesus only answered to keep silent about it.

The twentieth chapter of Matthew gives an interesting view of the cabinet-rank system. Jesus foretold his fate, saying, "I will not be a king; instead, I will be spat upon, be mocked, be scourged, and at last be crucified, and [yet] the third day I will rise again." His disciples, however, never took the prediction for the truth, but continued their quarrels for precedence, as if to answer, "Master, don't be silly!" They were absorbed in prosecuting their claims as to who would occupy the highest rank when the master formed his cabinet.

It was on this occasion that Jesus took up a little child in his arms and taught, saying, "Whosoever shall humble himself as this little child, the same is greatest in the kingdom of heaven." Nevertheless, the disciples could not easily rid themselves of the idea that the rank system applied in the Kingdom of Heaven as it did on earth. Accordingly, Jesus' secret of the Heavenly Kingdom remained unrevealed and unrealized until the end of his life.

(MATTHEW 16:12)

29

MEEKNESS

WHY was Jesus meek? The answer is that the most powerful force in the world is a mother's love. The sword may seem to avail more, but, after all, the sword is the frailest of man's weapons.

The sun shines upon the earth from a distance of 93,000,-000 miles. Ice as solid as a granite rock melts away like wax before its rays. So stubborn hearts and iniquitous social systems—though they may be dented by force—will dissolve in the embrace of love.

Eleven centuries elapsed after Jesus before the slaves in Europe were emancipated. Historians have given two reasons for this emancipation: (1) the Stoic doctrine of the equality of all men, and (2) the gospel of love promulgated by Jesus. Truly, the power of love melted away the iron chains of slavery. This is the strength of meekness. We might list innumerable examples of reforms of social systems where, although military means accomplished nothing, change was brought about by the example and practice of love.

Air is soft but elastic. Compressed in the air hammer, it can rivet and clinch iron plates. Blessed are the meek, for they possess elasticity. The meek shall inherit the earth, for they are flexible.

(MATTHEW 5:5)

30

THE STARTING POINT OF THE PRINCIPLE OF NONRESISTANCE

A COWARD who does not return a blow dealt him seems a poor-spirited fellow from a human point of view. But Jesus was charged with a duty to act by nobler principles, as God does. The root of the principle of nonresistance lies in the belief that death itself is not to be feared since God can rescue any man even though he appears to have been killed.

If one is not charged with a primary duty to save others, it is a loss and a folly to be moderate in all things. However, one who wants to save others must not fight back. One knows that the power of salvation is more than man's power. The principle of nonresistance of Jesus is composed of this transcendental faith. And one who cherishes the transcendental faith is obliged to believe in the ethics of nonresistance.

"Vengeance is mine; I will repay."

Judgment and punishment are the prerogatives of God. Man's part and task is to draw water from the wellspring of love that flows within. If our human societies are to evolve, all of us must practice from this very moment the rule of nonresistance by every means at our disposal.

(MATTHEW 26:51-53)

31

LOVE AS MELTING POWER

Such a religion as is merely preached by mouth and heard by outer ears will soon be denied. The genuine gospel is the religion which is preached by love. Love has the fusing power of the sun beaming upon ice. The solid Roman Empire melted away before this gospel. It was not, however, the dogma and the doctrine of Christianity that exerted this effect upon that imperial structure.

It was not Christianity that accomplished it, but love! Considered from the points of view of theory, the philosophy of Plato or Stoicism was far superior to Christian theology. Indeed, Christianity had recourse to the phrases of Plato or Stoicism to elaborate its own theology.

Synthetic theology can never rouse the hearts of men. Nothing short of love avails to that end. Theology is but an appendix to love, and an unreliable appendix! Love exists before theology can ever be thought of. Love does not come out of philosophy. No theology can be strictly called the theology of the Cross. I have no intention to disparage theology, but I do say it is no source of sufficient heat to melt the hard heart of humankind.

(Romans 12:10-15)

32

ONE WHO BEARS OTHERS' SINS

SUFFERINGS can be divided into two classes, the kind for which man should be held responsible, and the other for which God alone is responsible. We are not accountable for disasters, disease, age and infirmity, for the struggle for existence, because the structure of the universe causes these. For whatever enters the realm of his conscience, however, man is obliged to accept the full responsibility. Regardless of its defense of itself, any communistic society has attachments to the human conscience it cannot disavow. There are various forms of communistic life. Fleas, mosquitoes, and other insects practice a common ownership of property. Communism which repudiates man's conscience is, so to speak, the communism of ants. Before the common ownership of property on the human level, however, there must be mutual aid based on mutual love and the willingness to make self-sacrifice. Otherwise the system will never work. Communistic life, therefore, can never be established through a terroristic revolution. As a preliminary to it, a truth of conscience must be taught. This eternal truth was exhibited in Jesus' selection of self-sacrifice and a cross instead of a revolution. Ridiculous as it appears to many, no other way is available. Jesus chose alone a way unacceptable to the multitude. Nevertheless, he never cursed his antagonists, but assumed responsibility for others' as well as for his own decisions, a responsibility concerning not merely property but also acts of will. It seems almost fantastic, but in this wise he bore the sins of the world.

(MATTHEW 1:21)

33

VIA DOLOROSA

JESUS decided on the Cross rather than on a revolution. Nowadays the choice of revolution has become familiar and its results well known. But the suggestion of a cross is still treated with contempt and scorn. What is the sense of mentioning such an old-fashioned device as a cross? Jesus was deserted by the masses of his people. Today most people dismiss him just as lightly.

A cross! Can a cross possibly compete with a revolution? Someone may ask, If we really desire to serve mankind, why would we not exert ourselves directly for the emancipation of slaves, or for housing improvement, or for educational betterment, or for the relief of orphans? Why did Jesus do otherwise and embrace the Cross of his own volition? Were not all his efforts in vain? That they were not was Jesus' secret. The way Jesus took was by no means obvious to us moderns. His secret penetrated so deeply into the inwards of conscience that it strikes us still as a mystery. His way could be taken by none but the feeble-minded or the ignorant. This way bore Jesus straight to the Cross. But his example in pursuing it captures our souls today, nineteen hundred years later. The mystery is nothing but love! It is redemptive love! During these hundreds of intervening years many a disciple has been captured by this love of Jesus. And even today it is capturing our devotion.

(MATTHEW 27:31)

34

REVOLUTION? OR CROSS?

WHEN did Jesus determine to reveal his secret of the Cross? His decision was fixed when the question was raised by his disciples whether Christ would rebel against the Roman tyranny as the long-expected deliverer, or espouse some other method. He then let out his dark secret. John the Baptist, who had been in prison for accusing the wicked King Herod for his unlawful marriage with his brother's wife, was finally beheaded on the evening of the king's birthday, and his head given to Salome, beloved daughter of Herodias. At this time the masses were eager to rebel against Herod and assembled around Jesus. But he would never resign himself to that mission. He retired into a quiet place, then taught his followers, saying, "You think too simply. You think only of a passing revolution and not of eternity. You will starve that way, but you will lack no good thing my way." "Coward!" "Traitor!" "Blockhead!" Thus deriding him, the crowd of thousands dispersed in all directions. Seeing his disciples standing alone, Jesus asked them, saying, "Are you going to leave me, too?" Scarcely a dozen remained. Jesus forthwith made a journey with his twelve to the neighboring country, Phoenicia, and again returning home, at Caesarea Philippi, he revealed his secret for the first time, telling them, "I desire an eternal revolution instead of an ephemeral one." Despite the revelation, the disciples were unable to understand, until his death, what the Cross meant.

(JOHN 6:49)

35

THOSE WHO BELIEVE IN RESURRECTION

THE resurrection of Jesus had a far deeper significance than what happened to the flesh. It meant the resurrection of spirit beyond the needs of any carnal body. Therefore, it was not necessary for the disciples to see the resurrected Jesus, nor for the tomb-keepers to observe him. The Roman soldiers guarded the sepulcher lest his body should be stolen away, but they were not able to testify to his resurrection either. Much less were casual passers-by.

The first person to discover the resurrection of Jesus that morning was Mary Magdalene whose soul had once been possessed with seven devils. The resurrection of Jesus was a resurrection for such miserable persons as she, for ruined souls. To those who cannot grasp this meaning, resurrection remains an insoluble enigma, an empty falsehood, a prick of doubt. It is an everlasting secret. Not a few of us seem inclined to deny this miracle. If we are reluctant to accept sinners as our friends, it means that we belong to the skeptics who deny the fact of resurrection. Let us, therefore, remember that the first witness who saw the figure of Jesus the morning of his resurrection had been a prostitute.

(JOHN 20:1)

36

UPLIFT OF CONSCIENCE

THE essence of Jesus' religion is not its miraculous character. Miracles themselves did not constitute the religion of Jesus. It is a gross mistake to take his miracles for the essence of Christianity.

Jesus never made his miracle the central point of his teaching. He simply used this power as a means of manifesting his personality.

The salient feature of Jesus' religion is neither his virgin birth nor his resurrection. The gist of his religion is the uplift of conscience wrought through God and Christ. This implies that, recovering our benumbed divine sense, we enter into that sacred precinct where God and man are united, and there revel in the love of our Heavenly Father. This is the religion of Jesus.

The miracles were only an addendum, an afterthought.

Christianity would continue unimpaired even if all the miracles were to be completely eliminated from it. Nevertheless, it is a certainty that Jesus Christ could perform miracles, and did perform them. The only question for criticism to decide is how far we are to depend upon their acceptance.

(JOHN 11:43-44)

37

NEW CREATION

WHILE we were yet sinners, Christ died for us. So it is written in the epistles to the Romans. This is love. Some people are proud of having given little bits of charity to others, but such meager doles cannot represent true love.

This love of Christ cannot be understood by those who think only in the moral terms of give and take, who dwell only on the struggle for existence and its amelioration through mutual aid. The love of Christ has little to do with physiological and psychological consideration. It is his intention to restore the moral ruin at the bottom of a soul. Such love must utilize the power with which God originally created light out of darkness. That creative power is required to create a new soul out of the darkness of sin. Why then must sinners be forgiven? Redemption means that the ego is resmelted in the crucible that is Christ and poured forth anew. When this new creation appears, sins are dissolved and banished by this very process.

(ROMANS 5:8)

38

PERSONAL INTOXICATION

By creating human beings God gave Himself plenitude and abundance. By being His good children we add to God's glory. And let us reflect on the meaning of Glory. In the Gospel according to St. John are recorded many such experiences of glory. Jesus' prayer in the seventeenth chapter of St. John is a prayer of glory. For Jesus this word "glory" had a deep significance. The ultimate value of glory resides in personal contact. Our sole desire when we long to glory is to be with God. The joy we derive from being with a sweetheart is a kind of intoxication which comes from intimacy. Nothing can be more joyful than such personal intoxication. Our joy with our children, in the company of our loved ones, and much more the joy derived from our union with God—the joy of such companionship exceeds any power of description.

It is right that we have this joy with God, and of God. We must enter the eternal silence, expecting to behold the face of God.

This personal intoxication, this personal victory, this joy that nought else can give, is ecstasy, triumph, glory, and it is God Himself.

(JOHN 17:4)

39

PASSION

JESUS essayed to reconstruct this world with a flame of passion. Since he himself was a man of passion, Jesus had appreciation of, and sympathy for, the passions of others. When a prostitute who had been spurned by all the good people, knelt down, her adoration aflame, and anointed his feet with valuable ointment, Jesus did not chide her for her effrontery but accepted the token of her love.

This same Messiah showed he possessed another complement of passions, too. He was fierce in casting out the merchants who desecrated the temple. He drove out the cattle from the holy precincts, and overturned the tables of the money-changers. No mild and shrinking weakling was Jesus on this occasion.

It has been said that truth is no longer truth when it lacks zeal to enforce it. Only after thousands of futile experiments did Edison succeed in the invention of the electric light. Without passion for success, no social betterment movement will ever come to pass, nor will truth be enthroned.

Jesus was as passionate as one whose zeal has eaten his flesh. He overflowed with a godlike enthusiasm. It was because of his passion that Jesus lamented over the iniquity of the wicked and the depraved. He sighed over evil, when he looked up to heaven. Despite the passion that stirred in his bosom, however, Jesus cherished at the same time a crystal serenity in the depth of his soul and maintained a composure that no passion could destroy.

(LUKE 12:19)

40

MORE THAN PERSONAL PERFECTION

THE gospel of Jesus involves not only what is called spirituality, but also salvation. His gospel includes an assurance of perfect salvation physically, psychologically and morally; the salvation of body as well as of spirit. Jesus gave mysterious power to his disciples and ordered them to heal the sick, to raise the dead, to cleanse the lepers, and to cast out the evil spirits from those spiritually and mentally deranged. Only by following Jesus' examples were the disciples able to perform all four types of these wonderful arts.

Today churches have no such definite objectives. They lack any clear sense of the Kingdom of God. They aim mainly at the moral behavior of individuals, and are quite indifferent to such works as the healing of the sick, the raising of the dead and the cleansing of lepers. These duties no longer fall within the function of the Church. It is not thought to be the Church's business to revitalize the nation. But should Christianity not drive out the evil spirit of anarchy? Jesus said that the gospel of the Kingdom of God should be preached not only with the lips but with the deeds of the hand and the whole body. We must be evangelists of the Heavenly Kingdom, therefore, in factories, on farms and in hospitals, as well as preachers in church.

(JAMES 2:15-16)

41

LABOR

THERE are two types of revolution: one revolutionary idea is destructive, the other is productive. The former is exemplified by communism. The communist unhesitatingly lives on other people's property: confiscation is more to his taste than work. On the other hand, productive revolutionists are those who work with all their might whatever the social ideals they cherish.

The same two different trends can be distinguished in the ideas of Parousia, or Second Coming. Some of the Thessalonians had the notion of a destructive Parousia. These led an idle life and seem to have practiced a corresponding system of communism, whose watchword was one of despair. After all, this world will soon be consumed. Let's enjoy what we may before its destruction.

Paul, however, preached a gospel of labor, encouraging his followers to work hard, and assuring them that victory would surely come about by the virtuous. The Second Advent will take place when the productive revolution wins out. To idlers, the great day will never dawn. Their reward is an idle illusion. Therefore, we must work faithfully and steadily. God will finally grant productive people compensation for their toil and endurance, and rest in a world at peace. Until that time we must do our best in the labor assigned to us. Thus Paul teaches us and so he taught the Thessalonians.

(II THESSALONIANS 3:12)

42

ONE WHO LOVES ONE'S ENEMY

THE progress of civilization, in every age, requires that those in the van become victims in order that the masses may follow them. Forerunners who lead the procession must always undergo the experience of suffering. They must show patience and endurance. They must bless their assailants and those who curse. No man can lead others if he hates those that persecute him. The destruction of one's enemy retards one's own and everybody's progress.

However, if one sacrifices himself and lets his enemy flourish, power accrues to him who performs the sacrifice. The enemy lives, too, and within him the ability to love may be called into action. This anticipation of the enemy's growth in love is the motive for endeavoring to save him. In it the principle of loving one's enemy is rooted.

Bless them that curse you, do good to them that hate you, and pray for them that despitefully use you. It is vital and essential to keep this possible growth of the enemy in mind. If one envisages only the enemy's misdeeds there can be no motive for loving him. Our love for humanity insists that we take this attitude educationally and morally, from the standpoint of both economics and religion. Truly, the perfect society can be established only by those who strive to redeem their enemies, instead of exterminating them.

(MATTHEW 5:44)

43

SERVICE TO THE LEAST

JESUS never looked down on others. He taught his disciples to hold no person in contempt. A high degree of respect he paid particularly to children. During those old Roman times infants were subjected to a process we now call artificial selection. Likewise, in the Canton Provinces of China until fifty years ago, babies were abandoned according to their parents' whims. In India, too, a similar custom obtained of treating children cruelly. It was not until the coming of Jesus that those wicked practices were done away with, and children came to be respected as the hope of the future.

Why did Jesus reverence children? The reason is simple: they grow up, and contain more potent prospects of progress than adults do. Right here the principles and possibilities of education lie.

The aim of education has often been restricted to raising the pupil to the level of his teacher. But our aim must be to educate the new generation higher than the old. Should we not call this the evolutionary conception of education? It is more important to respect children, therefore, than to love them, to look forward to what they are to be.

The twentieth century may be called the century of children. Who, accordingly, are more to be revered than growing children whose muscles and souls alike are throbbing with activity? The teachings of Jesus foreshadow this shift from an adult-centered civilization to the child-centered one.

(MATTHEW 18:10)

44

AN IDEAL

TODAY there is an increased number of people who cherish communism as their ideal, but the type of communism thus coming into existence is woefully defective. Russia has established a Soviet-organized communism. But in order to carry out communism genuinely, there is no other way than for every man to return his possessions to God first of all. It is very important to give all our property back to God to whom everything belongs. Unless each of us has sufficient devotion to restore all things to God before we cry, "Workers, unite!" communism can never be a success. I do not believe that communism restricted to a single country can be called real and valid. To be real, communism must be changed into a God-centered undertaking. There is no other way to accomplish it. I often think that thieves maintain a kind of communism, too; that is, among themselves. So it can be said that there are two brands of communism: the God-centered type, and the thief type. It goes without saying that every genuine communist is seeking for God first of all. Paul dwelt on this condition. He expressed it in very marvelous words. According to him, Jesus Christ became poor, though he was rich, so that all men might be enriched through his poverty. If this ideal should be put into practice, heaven would descend upon earth. Dwelling upon this idea led Paul furthermore to declare that all men are made equal.

(II CORINTHIANS 8:9)

45

YET THERE IS ROOM

A CERTAIN criminal with several previous convictions once preached in a uniform of the Salvation Army. Though the preacher's own record was bad, not a few people were led to Christ through his sermons. Thus God employs even an evil man in His wonderful way for good. God knows manifold means of using any scoundrel whatever.

John Newton, the noted hymn writer, was once a member of the crew of a slave ship. The slaves were hunted in the low land of the Congo, roped together, and transported to Cuba to be sold. One-fifth of them usually died during the voyage. When these captive Negroes rebelled, they were mercilessly thrown into the sea. But the Newton who was engaged in this iniquitous traffic was suddenly converted and reformed. He became an earnest disciple of Jesus. Influenced by Wesley, he is now remembered as a renowned hymn writer.

There is always hope for any man. A gleam of hope shines even from the criminal, as it once shone from the man who threw slaves into the sea because they imperiled his boat during a storm.

This is the gospel. The gospel asserts, Never despair. There is always a future for him who is beset by despair, a brighter day for all in adversity or distress.

(LUKE 14:22)

46

THE GOSPEL OF THE CROSS

FROM the creation of the earth until today hundreds of millions of years are said to have elapsed. But human beings have not completely evolved yet and are full of imperfections. Nevertheless, their Creator has not destroyed them but continues in patience to forgive them. This creative patience we call God.

We, too, must strive to possess such patience as God exhibits through what we call love.

We might wish that each of us could trust his fellows as God does, that we might not be so easily disappointed in one another, and that we could keep on having patience for what we find amiss. We must resolve to break the hard shells of our intolerance however difficult long habit may have made the task.

If one plants a branch of a willow tree in the earth, the twig which seemed to have withered begins to bud. To glimpse possibility in what seems impossible to the ordinary sight—this I call religion or salvation, or the Cross. Jesus is certain to have risen from the dead. Thus I call it the gospel of the Cross to create the possible out of the impossible.

Let us live zestfully, believing in this, and continue to pray and seek that we may resemble the Perfect in wisdom and love.

(II CORINTHIANS 5:17-18)

47

NATURE IS THE REVELATION OF GOD

ONE hundred and fifty years ago, when Napoleon went to Egypt on a military expedition, he discovered a stone slab at a place called Rosetta at the mouth of the Nile. That stone slab had been inscribed in parallel lines with different kinds of writing—Greek letters and Egyptian hieroglyphics. At first nobody took those pictures for characters, but finally, after careful study using the known Greek as the clue, it was found that each of the pictures was a symbol.

To those without knowledge the meaning of any letter or character will be unintelligible. In order to read the huge hieroglyphs written on the face of the universe, we must employ our insight. To some, a mountain remains a mountain, a river remains a river, and a sea remains a sea; and it is beyond their comprehension that each of these objects possesses some further meaning. But a keener intelligence discovers that the Todo River, Mt. Hiei, a wayside stone, a twinkling star—everything has a hidden significance as well as the obvious one. We should discover the meaning concealed deeply within all nature. My desire is to acquire such comprehension of the universe through the exercise of spirit.

To a genuinely clear mind the letters written on the universe are distinctly legible. We must possess such a religious consciousness that we can read this invisible writing.

(PSALM 19:1)

48

GROWTH TO SANCTIFICATION

"SANCTIFY them through thy truth: thy word is truth." This is one of the prayers of Jesus (John 17:17). Though he uses the word "sanctification" here, he seldom uses it elsewhere.

At the age of seventeen I read the seventeenth chapter of the Gospel of St. John and learned much from it. But I did not dream that sanctification was possible for me. We freely talk of love or faith, but at the mere mention of sanctification, we feel somehow shy and hesitant. However, this culmination is the most beautiful sanctuary of religion. Unless it be reached, religion remains imperfect. This sanctification that Jesus referred to is far beyond our power to achieve. But strange it is, too, that buds burst out after the soft spring rain. Always when I look upon it, I am surprised at a pine-tree bud. I cannot help marveling at the birth of any new thing through the influence of the Holy Spirit. And I long within myself for the experience of the Holy Spirit.

When we are enfolded in the embrace of the Holy Spirit, the Holy Christ gradually enters us. It is due to the Holy Spirit that we feel gradually sanctified whether we walk in the field, or lie abed, or are managing a sum of money entrusted to us by others.

(I PETER 1:16)

49

AFFLICTION AND PATIENCE

At the coming of the spring, seemingly withered grass
sprouts and shoots forth from the earth. Spring comes similarly to our souls when they are dissipated, spent, or languish
in prison cells. Let people laugh at this if they wish. Since
we believe in Jesus on the Cross, and accept the authority
of his decision, we follow his steps. Jesus was the Son of
God. He knew whereof he spoke. The story of the Cross is
a supernatural event.

Let those be indifferent to the death of Jesus who find
they can be. But there are those, too, who accept the power
of rebirth when it is breathed into them so strongly through
the Cross. Since the time at the age of twenty-two when I
decided to make my career in the darkness of slums, I have
followed the example of Jesus seeking after his secret and
bidding farewell to the winter of sorrows. I have enjoyed a
perpetual springtime.

We should not be in despair over the miseries of Japan.
Resurrection through the Cross can come to us, too. We believe in the future that destroys death and breaks the coffin
of the past. Jesus experienced that triumph, leaving the
tomb behind. The Cross means that the eternal love tramples even death underfoot. Defeat, poverty and sin are not
stronger than the Cross.

(James 5:11)

50

UGLINESS AND THE CREATOR

SOME people get gloomy because of their ugliness. But not every feature of them can be ugly, however ugly they may be. By improving themselves here and there or eliminating offending trifles, they can be made beautiful to anyone's satisfaction. Concerning the treatment of ugliness, it is necessary to know two ways to proceed: (1) elimination of the unwanted and (2) the positive power of beauty itself. The peacock's tail exhibits beautiful patches, but these were originally ugly spots and have turned out to be beautiful only through scores of generations of selection. Compared with the generation of their grandparents, children today are far superior. The painter, Whistler, wrote an essay entitled *10 P.M.* which said that at ten o'clock at night even muddy water gleams with the reflection of light. From London Bridge at 10 P.M. the river which looked ugly in the day loses its filth as the Thames reflects the glow of gas lights. The surface of the muddy city stream is beautified at night as it sparkles with the gems of light. Whatever imperfections exist on earth, we are able to get rid of through social influence working gradually through many long years. A new 10 P.M. is bound to come to society.

(ROMANS 9:20-21)

51

HIGH TIDE FOR SOULS

THE power to tide one over all the sorrows in existence—sickness, old age and death—is gained through Christ. Thus our souls can be beautifully sculptured. But unless we remember the name of our Lord in the days of our youth, there is no hope for us to get started in a spiritually worthy life. I am thinking of Mr. Cleveland, a former President of the United States. One day Cleveland and a friend of his, a lawyer, were walking on the street, when they happened to pass by a church. Cleveland went into the church, while his friend bade him farewell and directed his own steps toward a bar. From that point on, this friend's path led downward until finally he found himself confined in the jail of a southern city, Dallas. At this time he read the report that Cleveland was inaugurated as President. The one man who had turned his face toward God rose higher and higher, while the other who had failed in the moment of choice fell lower and lower, until he reached the depths in jail. The first step made a big difference. If our present course is tending upward, we will never decline even when others fall by the wayside. But we must be alert for the initial chance. We must watch out for beginnings.

At the age of thirty or forty, men's souls harden. This we might call the sclerosis of the spirit. It is too late to repent when one's heart has become as solid as a rock.

(REVELATION 22:10)

52

AMENDMENT OF THE UNIVERSE

A YOUNG man once said to me, "I would like to believe, but the temptation of death has captured my heart and never leaves me." I replied, "I, too, was once victim to such a pessimistic mood. But then it occurred to me that there still was one redeeming element in my heart. It was a conviction that there still remains in me a power to better the situation even though it be only a trifling bit. All external things may loom dark and forbidding, but as long as the strength to grasp a handful of sand remains, I must not give up my effort to amend the world"—so I thought.

Supposing that God Himself were to seem evil to me; as long as life exists I must continue my endeavors to amend that evil God. I firmly resolved, as long as conscience persists, to have the courage to challenge fate, to defy the law of cause and effect even if I am cast down into hell for my daring. I must strive for the advancement and amendment of the universe.

People are often liable to abandon their duty, declaring "God has forsaken me," or "I am exhausted with the battle of life." But even when the temptation of suicide beckons to us, we ought not to reject a single ray of hope that issues from the good.

(II CORINTHIANS 4:8-9)

53

GOD'S DEMOCRACY

"FOR ye see your calling, brethren, how that not many wise men after the flesh, not many mighty, nor many noble, are called: but God hath chosen the foolish things of the world to confound the wise; and God hath chosen the weak things of the world to confound the things which are mighty; and base things of the world, and things which are despised, hath God chosen, yea, and things which are not, to bring to nought things that are" (I Corinthians 1:26-28).

No stronger advocates of democracy can be found than the writers of the Bible. From what source springs the need of humbling ourselves? The reason is that God uses the weaklings of the world in order to overturn the mighty. He chooses the unlearned in order to confound university professors and the so-called wise. Jesus did not orate upon theories of faith in his farewell speech. He simply pronounced the words "Ye love one another," when he was captured and led away to court.

If we are defeated, it must be due to our lack of love. Where love is pure, it is potent and there a victory follows spontaneously. We have been called by God as those who have a duty to show forth the highest standard in our daily life in Japan. We should exhibit before the multitudes the example of Jesus' love.

(JOHN 13:14)

54

CHRIST AND DARWINISM

THE evolution of man implies that man leaves evil behind and advances to a higher and better level, that he gets rid of illusion and attains to truth. These strides can be realized only by an inner power and direction. Therefore, in the case of humanity, the idea of evolution assumes the employment of conscience. The human race can evolve only into the sons of God. Any person can become greater and nobler than he is now; it was Jesus who taught this. Accordingly, Christianity is a doctrine of evolution, the only type possible at this stage of development.

Man does not evolve only according to the rule of natural selection, but also by his own power of inner selection. This I call his conscience; it is his prerogative of moral selection. Man achieves progress by the help of God, being stimulated and energized from the inside. He is able to rise from his present low estate to a superior form by God's power working in him. Whatever provides a challenge to him, man must accept and respond to. His mind must be devoted to the pursuit of beauty, of good, of truth, everywhere in the universe. This is to ascend to another and a higher level. It becomes possible only when we feel a great power stirring within our souls. We must strive in order to advance. If we are madly in love with the objects of physical sense, being absorbed in instinct and pleasure, we are doomed to halt on the road of evolution.

(II CORINTHIANS 3:18)

55

THE PRINCIPLES OF GROWTH

JESUS caused everything to grow. Jesus came to fulfill the law and not to destroy it. No jot nor tittle should in any wise disappear from the law.

In China today, destruction is going on at a furious rate. Nothing is left but the roof tiles of the museum of Nanking. Lately I went to Nanking expecting to see what the remnants of the civilized Chinese in the T'ang Dynasty would look like. But to my regret, everything had been destroyed and my expectation was not fulfilled. On the contrary, returning to Japan and going to Nara, I found all of the excellent Chinese works of art there. The Japanese are superior by nature in having preserved these relics in good condition.

Now the Japanese have Christianity, and by adding their good impulses to it, they will be baptized by Christianity in a real sense. Christianity teaches there is no need of destroying anything that pertains to the present age. Everything should grow into fruition. Jesus exhorted us to be like unto him. Furthermore he told us that we would do greater works than his. The essence of the Kingdom of God is a principle of perpetual growth.

(MARK 4:31-32)

56

LOVE AND ECONOMY

IN social life human beings meet and love one another through a material medium. When we think we love, but fail to express the sentiment in tangible form, by some physical means, that love is not genuine nor complete.

"If a brother or sister be naked, and destitute of daily food, and one of you say unto them, Depart in peace, be ye warmed and filled; notwithstanding ye give them not those things which are needful to the body; what doth it profit?" Thus wrote James, the brother of Jesus.

Love spins garments for itself out of matter. Love which is not displayed physically is only partial and faulty. When love assumes the symbol of substantial existence, the economic life appears as the content of the spiritual. This relation may be the cause of a mistaken idea that economic activity can give birth to love. Life, however, is prior to its embodiments. It is an opposite error to think that economics deals only with material things. True economics must consider the purposes of life and regard matter as something meaningful. Economics is the art of living.

Art must create externally beautiful objects, and internally it is love itself. If we view economics so, the study of it changes into a science of love.

(HEBREWS 13:1-3)

57

THE BUSY GOD

JESUS says, "My Father worketh hitherto, and I work." My religion lacks no feature of an internal combustion engine. My God is a dynamic force. My God is an inventor, He is a God of action. My God is a God of adventure, and a Worker of miracles. He inspires man to prosecute adventures of his own and to perform miracles before He Himself does them. Existence is a miracle, a recurring mystery, and perpetually a wonder. God has the power of a hurricane. He takes away all weakness from my life. My God is an Accomplisher of marvels.

There may be a pastoral religion for people who like to be quiet and undisturbed. There may be a kind of religion which is nourished on indolence and a false peace of mind provided by the exertions of someone else. That religion may do for others, but I will have nothing to do with it. My God heats the sun to the temperature of 6,000 degrees. He causes the earth to rotate in twenty-four hours. My God is busy. He observes the laws that govern His creation. God is punctual. God is needed by every businessman. A god who is of value only in churches and cathedrals is of no use to me.

(JOHN 5:15-18)

58

A CROWD AND A MIRACLE

In a crowd of people a stronger power is generated than in these individuals by themselves. A crowd always expects a miracle. A multitude senses keenly that it can do nothing well without a great force intervening. In any age, no separate person acts so blindly and is so superstitious as the crowd. A group of men is ready to believe in anything.

In the midst of World War I a rumor prevailed that Christ appeared in visible form and toured the battlefields to comfort the wounded of the French, British and American armies. No reporter could confirm that the figure was really Christ himself. But all agreed that when they were in dire necessity, a strange Christlike person visited them to bring consolation. An amazingly large number testified that they had seen that visitor.

When people are driven to desperation and find themselves unable to get out of their plight by themselves, they are prepared to expect some miracle. No wonder then that people believed in such events when eight million fell in battle during the last World War.

It is quite natural that we turn to the miraculous when we sink into the depths of misfortune. Let us hope that we never become so hard-hearted and prosperous that we reject all possibility of a miracle.

(Mark 3:10-12)

59

ENOUGH COURAGE TO SHED BLOOD

THE "Kingdom of God" is a movement—one in which the blood of the Lamb flows into us, and in which our own blood is shed in the fight for the same cause. Therefore, patience is necessary to it. We have to overcome hardships by doing our utmost. In the extremity of our pain, we cry out in a loud voice, "How long dost Thou not judge and avenge our blood on them that dwell on the earth?" But God replies, "Be patient and wait for a little while." Many of our fellow workers and friends have died for this cause. In our grief and resentment we feel like demanding, "O, Lord, how long do you not avenge? How long shall you leave us alone?" But God's command we hear again, "Enough people have not been killed. The blood of sacrifice is not sufficient. Be patient until more misfortunes come. Wait until the blood of sacrifice covers the whole world, then the blood which is shed for the work of salvation will be sufficient."

In Japan, the Kingdom of God cannot come until more blood is poured out. We must not leave this outpouring to God's ministers. We must shed our own blood. We must not sleep. Our duty is to walk the way of the Lamb who was obedient and gave His blood. Do we have courage equal to the shedding of blood? Or do we not? The blood that is called for is not to be understood as the blood of slaughter, but the blood that we offer for the sake of Japan.

(REVELATION 2:10)

60

A HUMAN BULLET

God has made me into a bullet and is aiming to shoot it at a certain target. This is the sentiment of Jesus, perfectly expressed. "Nevertheless, not as I will, but as thou wilt." His whole self was propelled according to God's will—flying to the destination fixed by Him, his own will abandoned. Jesus is the best example we can cite of such integrity. Jesus sped along in line with God's will. He was shot exactly as God had aimed.

Thus, once we have accepted the spirit of the whole universe as our own, we will not be diverted even by poverty, by imprisonment, by loneliness, or by death. We take our position within the God of the universe. God's purpose is animating the universe. This purpose is steady and cannot be deflected. Even though we sometimes waver in performing our part, His purpose for us has already been fixed.

Once we realize what this purpose is, we never fear tempests or contrary winds. We merely march forward along our destined way despite all obstructions. If we renounce our own self wills and yield ourselves to the will of the universe, we find living easy and pleasant. Ours is that calm state of mind known as religion. We are then like bullets which are discharged by the hand of God.

(PHILIPPIANS 1:14)

61

BLESSINGS IN JAIL

EVEN though I were thrown into jail a hundred times,
And its bars should confine me for a hundred years,
Never would my will relax, no never!
Never till the day of liberty dawns again for me.
I will hold fast to my present resolution.
Into my prison cell brightly beams the morning sun,
— O God, on the window, on the roof,
— On wooden fences, on iron bars, and on my stool.
Lord, my prison cell is a garden full of flowers.
How absurd it is to arrest one who dwells in God.
My soul is speeding with the light of the rising sun
From east to west, to south and to north,
Flying about over all the surface of the world.
In my prayers I forget my prison cell oftentimes,
And forget myself,
And that is why I am thankful for the happiness of God.

(ACTS 16:25-31)

62

"EDUCATIONAL SOCIALISM"

I ENTERTAIN but slight hope of saving any poor people above
the age of twelve. The laboring classes may discover some
device to liberate themselves tentatively by labor unions.
But it is almost impossible to save those poor folks who can
scarcely get along without being dependent on others and
who are physically and psychologically deficient.

Therefore, in my opinion, the way to get rid of poverty is
to devote our attention to children before they are rendered
helpless. And the way to save them is to give them a truly
creative education and to plan it so that they may not only
be able to live independently as adults but to produce from
their own ranks excellent men as leaders.

I would accordingly lay the foundation of every social
movement on educational socialism.

I believe that by proceeding this way, we can build the
good society in which our souls never stoop and cringe before dictatorial authority. The masses must be liberated by
the spirit of love and mutual aid. We can hope to be freed
from past errors only by the cultural sciences. Then we can
live in the realm of high ideals, abjuring the use of force,
and realizing the dream of reconstruction.

(LUKE 2:34-35)

63

LOVE AND LABOR

I WELL know that strikes and walkouts and such manifestations of the class struggle are not going to solve the problem in the least. Still, enforced labor under the capitalistic system, I know, too, is even less satisfactory. The basic problem is the lack of love. Love can be expressed in no other way than through labor. Labor is an embodiment of a volition, and love is its goal. The completion of love is impossible without labor, and labor without love is empty and burdensome. The very day when love and labor unite, mankind will achieve a perfect social life. Only labor can maintain society intact.

However, labor destitute of love plunges the worker into hell. Love is the reformer we are always looking for; love is the perennial revolutionist. Furthermore, love is a permanent ally of labor. Only love can cement society together. Society is integrated by love. Any economy must be judged according to the density of its love. The credit system, facilities of transportation, communication and manufacture, all are good or bad, strong or weak, according to the measure of the love they contain. Love rejuvenates any society and keeps it strong and virile.

Reconstruct with love. Purify with love. Love is the eternal revolutionist.

(I JOHN 4:12)

64

THE HAND OF SALVATION

CALL the best God! There's no mistake about it. Call the most beautiful God! There's no mistake about that, either. Call the truest God! You are right, again! The true, the good and the beautiful are correctly known as God. However, the good cannot be called God if it is only good and nothing more. It is because of its power to change evil into itself, we call the good, God. Since there is a power that beautifies the ugly, straightens the crooked, purifies the filthy, cheers the broken-hearted, and summons everybody to salvation, we call that power God. One might call a way stretching straight ahead by the name, evolution. But God is more than a mere way, God is the power of salvation. Of this I am sure. Who else can comfort me when my soul is cast down, wounded, grieving and embittered? Evolution will say, I will leave you behind. Scientific law will tell you, You are excluded from my domain. And nature will say, I am cold-hearted. However, when both the wise and the foolish of the world open their mouths to abuse me for my stupidity, look! the hand of salvation is outstretched to me. Whose hand can it be but God's? Whose else but the Creator of my life and my merciful Father?

(LUKE 23:43)

65

HOLDING TO THE TRUTH

LOVE is the manifestation of an organism. It is the whole body that loves. Each cell in the body does not think of its own self-interest nor is it indignant when its interest is denied. The nails and hairs never get provoked when they are trimmed off and cast away for the sake of the welfare of the whole. In any organism, love requires that every member renounce its self-interest and does not get angry when called upon to sacrifice itself.

Love does not rejoice in iniquity, but rejoices in the truth.

However, on some occasions, love is liable to fall into iniquity on account of its excess. Love should not love too much and must always respect the demands of truth and justice. We call it rationalization when love makes out that it is above equity. But this is a distortion of the true situation, and self-deception.

True love ought to be always righteousness and to be the truth.

The greatness of Mahatma Gandhi, that leader of the Hindu revolution, lay in his philosophy that "holding to the truth is true love." We must always respect the clear light of fact and hold to the truth.

(I CORINTHIANS 13:5-6)

66

PEACE OF MIND

PEOPLE are busy today from morning till night counting figures and adding up accounts. Thus they have no peace in their minds. Most men are nothing but profit-reckoning machines. Through their veins a typhoon is blowing continuously and a depression is always circulating between their head and heart.

Peace of mind can never be purchased with money. In the summer of the tenth year of Taisho (1921), in the crisis of the labor-management dispute, I could keep peace of mind within myself. It was only because this peace was sent by God. I was praying, though my eyes were open, amid the excitement of that dispute.

Gandhi, the Indian philosopher, was a possessor of this peace of mind. He had an idea, formed by a combination of the teachings of Brahmanism, the thought of Ruskin and Tolstoy, advocating the philosophy he called "the realization of life." This idea emphasized the calm grasp of truth. Indeed, with this peace of mind in his grasp, Gandhi could resist the great British Empire, leading three hundred million Indians with him.

Truth is always the source of peace of mind. Jesus was the fountain of peace as he was of truth. Accordingly, he showed not a trace of fear. Even in the midst of the storm he quieted the fear and trembling of his companions with his words, "Be of good cheer. Be not afraid." And again he taught them, "Fear not, little flock."

(LUKE 12:32)

67

RELIGION AS A LIFE

RELIGION is not a theory but a life. It requires that we experience God every moment. Religion is not born by magic when we are baptized, but it is engendered when we become conscious of it. In other words, religion is not to be had by being taught about it, but must be experienced afresh by each person.

So, when we try to teach children a religion which is suited to the experience of adults of mature years, it is utterly impossible for children to grasp it. The result is that children will never experience religion in their entire lifetimes. Fortunately, religion is no thing to be passed on secondhand.

Not only the priests of Zen sect grasp religion immediately but people who lived two thousand years before the appearance of Zen sect possessed this sort of religion. Accordingly, it would be better today to give children the religion adapted to children. This may be a religious experience similar to that of primitive people who were not ashamed of their nakedness in the Garden of Eden. Our present practice is that doctrines or ceremonies which are too difficult even for adults to understand are forced on children, so children flee at the mention of religion, instead of being attracted to it.

(I JOHN 1:2-3)

68

JOINT RESPONSIBILITY

WHEN we live together in society, we have to accept responsibility for others. When society is stained with sin, each one of us must assume that sin. This is redemptive love. Those who do refuse and reject this joint responsibility cannot be members of this society. Unless we bear the consequences of others' faults even when these others show indifference, we do not possess the spirit of social solidarity. For this spirit is a spirit that strives for redemption.

A good society does not come into existence until this sense of redemptive love makes its appearance. Modern civilization exhibits a selfish trend which seems to hate others' defects and aims at a good society on one's own terms. But Jesus always declared that social responsibility was joint. "All things whatsoever ye would that men should do unto you, do ye even so unto them" (Matthew 7:12).

Indeed, this idea is Jesus' fundamental rule for social organization. The moment the sense of mutual aid has vanished from us, our society is doomed to fall apart.

In the Christian conception we must assume responsibility for both the good and the bad in our fellow men.

(HEBREWS 9:11-14)

69

INTO THE WORLD OF DESTINATION

IT is in order to possess now the world as it is destined to be that we believe in religion. Of course, we find something there we cannot understand. We do not know how such miracles as the resurrection of the dead or the healing of the blind were brought about. We cannot determine how far God's power had entered Jesus, nor how much of Jesus' power was human. However, our ignorance gives us no right to deny the fact. Though we have no intention to force all the accounts of the Bible on others as authentic, yet we enforce admission that there are unexplainable happenings in the world. At any rate, it is a fact that there does exist a mysterious realm in which every face is radiant. And I am eager for this element of mysteriousness to increase ever more. Can we not hope to have a world in which there are no sick people, no poverty-stricken people, no guns, no bombings? Are quarreling and fighting alone in accordance with natural law, and are fellowship and harmony to be regarded as unnatural? We pray that humanity may abolish war and that there will no more be machines made for slaughter. If the world of war and murder is natural, then we must set about to construct a supernatural world.

If such degradation is the only thing natural, I demand a supernatural world in which it ceases. The miraculous order of Christianity is the realm where the possibility of life is believed in.

(EPHESIANS 2:16)

70

EVOLUTION AND FAITH

I WILL not pry into the manner of how the amoeba has evolved into the form of man. If it did so naturally, it is quite simple that the amoeba was wiser than the scientist who explains it so easily. If it evolved by chance, nothing is more systematic and farsighted than chance. If it did so mechanically, there is no means to overcome the complex difficulties and to act with high spirits toward a freely conceived end better than machinery.

The faith in evolution is a daring faith when we survey it. It implies a firm belief that an electron can become a Son of God even if the stone cannot be turned into a son of Abraham. No faith is so optimistic, so remedial and so inspiring as that of evolution.

On the level of nature, evolution has revealed to us the inner power of potentiality. It is a faith that by the action of this inner power, the latent character of dust is transformed into the image of God unnoticed. Evolution teaches, in reality, a doctrine of progress and betterment. What a hopeful faith! Even if growth is destined to pass through the painful path of a struggle for existence, evolution guarantees a paradise at the end of the suffering. Evolutionism is full of hope. It is an ally, not an enemy, of religion.

(ACTS 17:26)

71

THE REAL SOCIAL ORGANIZATION

HERE are the novel good tidings. The gospel consists in the power of bringing the wounded and the dead to life. Here lies the mission of Jesus, the bearer of the message.

He said, "I came to call sinners to repentance," and this means, "It is my mission to reconstruct what has utterly been destroyed." This is Jesus' religion.

Jesus had a distinctive function. It was to declare God's plan to revive and to restore the declining civilization and corrupt society of that day instead of sweeping away their ruins.

God makes unceasing effort to join together again the broken pieces of the earthen vessel. Christianity is the religion in which this zeal of God has been proclaimed through the words and deeds of Jesus. Some people do not like the promise of this grace of God, and say, "I am in favor of righteousness only. The establishment of social justice will suffice. Let the evil be abolished."

However, Jesus said that God has the will to suffer for the sake of injustice as well. Unless you experience such suffering, too, you cannot have a part in the ideal Kingdom.

(ROMANS 5:20)

72

THE HEALTHY RELIGION

THE religion of Jesus originally was quite simple. Alto-
gether too simple, it may seem to many people somehow
unreliable. As a matter of fact, the religion of Jesus can
actually be grasped and shared by any man.

Those whose minds are complex affairs say that they do
not believe in Jesus' religion as there are no theories contained in it. But theories are never the essential to living
religion. In order to live, we need no particular theories
about life. Theories are later additions when life is beginning to fail.

Jesus made a religion of life exactly as he experienced it.
He never mentioned the names of Plato, Aristotle or the
Stoic school of philosophy prevailing in those days. On the
contrary, he illustrated his preaching with simple parables.
Sixty-four parables can be counted in the Gospel according
to St. Matthew alone. St. Mark writes that "without a parable spake he not unto them." There is an account of the
temptation besides those parables in the first Gospel, and
this record may be also a parable into which the valuable
experience of Jesus was embedded. The religion of Jesus
shows many colors and views. The Gospel is a rich and vital
view of living expressed, therefore, wholly in parables.

(MATTHEW 11:25-27)

73

THE REVOLUTIONARY NATURE
OF LOVE

ANY cure for human ills proposed by philosophy must regard nothing but love. Our Kingdom-of-God movement must of course betake itself into the sphere of philosophy. But salvation even philosophically considered must be achieved by love. We should not neglect such philosophy as lies within our reach, in our endeavors to seek the way. Why is there one religion that has persisted during these two thousand long years? The reason is that it is a religion of conscience. Love is eternal. We proclaim the immortality of love rather than the conservation of energy. Evolution implies nothing but the manifestation of love. We must step from one hill of love to another, and not plod along the valleys.

When we achieve love in its heights, we have got rid of all afflictions. All fear whatever has been banished. The socialistic movement is after all an evolution of love. Anarchism, or communism, or labor unionism cannot be made a success of by people who have no love. No movement is more adventurous than love. Love alone is truly revolutionary.

However, love is conservative at the same time, since it leaves all order intact. Love creates the most perfect of all organizations. The Church must be an organization of love. All organizations indeed are held together by the love generated by the invisible Church. Love will be finally victorious, and its power must be transmitted to the home and to society. This is the goal to which every movement must be directed.

(MATTHEW 7:12)

74

EDUCATION LEADING UP TO CONSECRATION

Needless to say, it is by no means easy for religious education to fulfill its task. This same judgment must be rendered concerning Christian Sunday schools and with regard to theological seminaries. Sunday schools today place too much emphasis on instruction in history and similar branches and do not provide the educational movement with the stimulus of great consecration which I advocate. Their methods are too exclusively intellectual.

Education in theological seminaries is defective in the same manner. Devoutness is not taught, but merely doctrines and dogmatic notions concerning the universe. Such one-sided intellectual education results in the drying up of character, and in the loss of interest in the creation of value. Students are too liable to forget that the essence of every value movement is to become a friend of sinners or of the rank and file. Ministers, moreover, get to nursing a mistaken idea that being a scholar is itself religion. Thus, religion is emasculated and becomes a social curse, rather than a cure for curses. This condition is not due to any evil inherent in religion but to the apathy of so-called religious people.

(Luke 2:11-52)

75

LOVE SUCCEEDS

PAUL, the apostle of Jesus, wrote to the Christians of the church at Corinth, "The more abundantly I love you, the less I be loved, but nevertheless I will very gladly spend and be spent for you." Paul was acting on a conviction that when love is active inside society, that love is sure to be consummated because it accords with the plan that God has arranged beforehand. Since he had this faith, Paul drew the conclusion, "Because it was to be given, I sought for it."

Love is the fuel of the social power plant. It warms the body from inside. Suppose we throw coals onto the earth, can the earth really be warmed? In other words, will society improve through my love? Many people question this effect of love. But if we let Paul answer, he would say that love was bound to succeed though it might take time for success to be disclosed. Someday the person appealed to through love is sure to respond. Let us, therefore, not waver in our hope. When we start with love, we are inclined to be moderate in our expectations and demands for a response without despairing. Christian is the name of the most courageous person in this respect.

(ACTS 4:34)

76

THE JOYFUL WORLD

Is not the glow of an electric light, or the existence of the eye that beholds it, a miracle? Every moment I am thrilled that I have come into such a wonderful world. I peer into the faces of other people, and feel keenly what marvels we live in the midst of.

Some thinkers affirm that a miracle is an exhibition of natural law. But I say that a miracle falls in the field of faith. It comes to pass in response to the demands of man's free will asking to have it done this way, and relying on God's free will to do it. A miracle is the fruition of ardent love accomplished through a personality devoted to love like that of Jesus.

God links together the events of our lives. I believe it. God fills the gaps within human effort. History is, therefore, a record of the miracles that God has performed on behalf of mankind. Consequently, we can never believe in miracles unless we believe first in His supernatural power. This belief is necessary if we are to find the world joyful. Through it we can always take a faithful attitude, trusting in God who loves the weak, and in the intervention of His power; that is, in a miracle.

(PSALM 40:5)

77

HERE I AM!

To the voice of the Lord, asking, "Whom shall I send?" the prophet Isaiah answered and said, "Here I am; send me." Twelve-year-old Samuel who was sleeping in the temple at midnight, when he heard the voice of God calling, "Samuel! Samuel!" immediately responded, "Here I am!"

Is each of us ready to answer, "Here I am!" when we hear God's voice now? Are we prepared to give a definite answer, "Yes, here I am!" to the question, "Are you there?" Are we really aware of our own existence? Dare we go out leaving everything behind us? Are we ready for that? Is ours the same courage as that of the first apostles who followed Jesus, turning their backs on the world?

When the summons comes, "Hello, everybody, are you there?" are not our clothes or shoes the whole of us? Are we really existing as persons that God can address? "Are you there, everybody?" God exists and He is speaking. Religion appears when an existent man meets God. God is what exists, and we must partake of existence, too. One who is destitute of heart and root is not alive. We are instead all indispensable and needed. Whatever our station in society, we can all be human beings.

(ISAIAH 6:8)

78

THE POWER WORKING BEHIND
THE HISTORY

SINCE poverty is not primarily the fault of individuals but is due to inequities of social organization, we have no cause to be pessimistic, I think. On the contrary, we have only to take courage and to reorganize society to procure the betterment of the world. Society now faces such a reconstruction; without this treatment, society can hardly endure. Concerning this prospect, I am not at all pessimistic. Here the wonderful salvation of God is moving behind and assisting our endeavors. The extension of social justice will hasten the day when the wealthy who are now proud of their possessions and who are now leading a life of vanity and idleness, will be put to shame. The movement toward democracy has been ascendant and victorious, never yielding an inch backward, for the last four centuries. When Martin Luther proclaimed the freedom of conscience, in opposition to the authority of the Pope, who could see he wielded any power? But strange to say, he did win! The popular crusade by John Calvin in Switzerland, Cromwell's movement in England, the American and the French Revolutions, the success of which laid the foundation of government in modern times, brought about a trend to democracy in economic affairs. We cannot resist the thought that some wonderful power is working behind this history.

(PSALM 145:21)

79

SORROWS AND JOY

IN our superficial world of today we find little spirit to laugh heartily. But Jesus foretold that the time will come when we can laugh, once we get rid of the impediments. He said, "Blessed are they that weep now: for they shall laugh." In order to laugh genuinely, instead of in a frivolous manner, we must first pursue the way of the truth.

In the prayer before his crucifixion, Jesus said, "These things I speak in the world, that you might have my joy fulfilled in yourselves." Again he taught his disciples that they should rejoice and be exceeding glad when they were persecuted, since their reward would be great in heaven.

A cheerful spirit—this is the religion of Jesus. The teachings of Jesus showed the way of renovation whereby we can discover a realm of joy in our present state. Since Christianity in our time preaches the Cross only, religion is considered to be exclusively a matter of sorrow, and our single prayer is "O God, forgive our sins." But this tone implies that we do not sense the other side of Jesus' religion. We cannot boast that we have mastered the true teachings of Jesus until we know the other side, that of the new birth by which a bud shoots out under the snows of earth at the cheerful warmth of the spring.

We, too, should return to God through Jesus after having shaken off our conventional garments.

(JOHN 17:13)

80

DISREGARD FOR THE TEMPLE

It is said that the temple of Jehovah in Jerusalem was built according to the Grecian style of architecture and that it cost one hundred million dollars and took forty-six long years to be completed. Marble was used lavishly in its construction. Its splendor was so impressive that the Jews forgot the wickedness of Herod and admired the grandeur of his handiwork. Jesus, however, said to his disciples who were admiring it, "Destroy this temple and in three days I will raise it up."

Did Jesus have no appreciation of architectural beauty? Yes! to be sure, he had. Jesus was a carpenter and a craftsman. Concerning architecture he had a knowledge equal to anybody's. But he had a keener aesthetic feeling for the art of life, more delight in the building of a human temple, than in the Jerusalem structure. He exulted in the beauty of life itself. Jesus could appreciate the truest of the arts.

The career of Jesus was a work of art designed by God. It was itself the perfection of religion, the beauty of a man whose soul and body exist in union and harmony. The influence which issued from this art became the power of resurrection and the forgiveness of sins.

Just as a grain of wheat germinates under the winter snow, so the soul must rise from its blanket of flesh. This very art is the most exalted element of Jesus' mission. Through God, Jesus has accomplished this noble work of art. It is poetry and life in one.

(JOHN 2:19)

81

THE DURABILITY OF LOVE

PERSEVERANCE is a quality inseparable from love. Parents persevere for a score of years in bringing up their children.

Dr. Warfield, a professor in Princeton Theological Seminary, never deserted his bride who was crippled for life by the accident of a runaway horse on her way home from the wedding. For years he kept this crippled wife in his study on a wheel chair and tenderly took care of her. Love alone can inspire a man to endure such a misfortune and to outlast the tragedy that inflicted it. Love endures and is durable to the end.

It is love that is the support and the foundation of the earth. Love is the groundwork of every organization. We should have within ourselves this durability of love. Ours must be the love that can endure through all sufferings. Jesus told us to love to the end. Love acknowledges no end. We must manifest this quality in our love. Love sacrifices everything that interferes. Love must persist as long as life itself. Love is as unchangeable as the spirit that sustains all things.

(II THESSALONIANS 3:3-5)

82

SLEEP

TEMPESTS rose from time to time on the Sea of Galilee. Jesus and his disciples encountered one of these storms when they were crossing the sea to the eastern coast. Matthew describes the scene as follows: ". . . insomuch that the boat was covered with the waves, but Jesus was asleep." Jesus was sleeping when this great storm arose. Sleep is one of the most precious gifts from Heaven. When I was eighteen years of age I often wondered why God had created sleep. I wished to be like God, who is perpetually awake and active. But as I grew older, I came to accept sleep with gratitude. It was not because I outgrew my desire to be constantly awake, but because I gained insight also into the nature of being a man. Man requires sleep, but refreshed through that means, he may awake with many times the vigor of a goldfish that does not sleep at all. Now that I have learned to enjoy life, I have ceased to complain to God on account of the necessity for sleep. I have learned that it is more significant to be satisfied with the enjoyment of sleep. Thus I can bear my burdens on a strong body, and that is better than to be always awake, but forever tired and full of complaints.

(MATTHEW 8:23-27)

83

NONVIOLENT LOVE

NONRESISTANCE does not imply cowardice. It means that we do no hurt to others.

Some misunderstand the intention of nonresistance, and take it for the approval of evil, or compromise. But this view is a gross mistake. Nonresistance directs us to stop our ineffectual meddling, and ineffectual it must be, if we do not reject evil fundamentally.

Love is a process of perpetual evolution. Life evolves without complaining of the sacrifice. If the sacrifice is not begrudged, social evolution will be better furthered in one's being killed than in killing.

Those who fear making the sacrifice love demands are compelled to fight. Those who have faith in the value of sacrifice, embrace the principle of nonviolence.

Deeply enshrined in evolution, there is the everlasting Cross.

Love is essential for the birth of the new society, while violence destroys every possible social organization.

Love is positive in its effect, while violence is negative.

Nonviolent love is permanently creative, while violence is degeneration, and works its own ruin.

(LUKE 23:33-34)

84

THE INVINCIBLE POWER OF FAITH

MIRACLES can be perceived only by those who believe. Miracles never produce conviction in those that doubt. If the problem of the miracle is to be settled on the basis of knowledge alone, skepticism will always be the answer. The power, however, that lifts a man from the depths of life has nothing to do with knowledge. That power makes connection with his will and affections.

It is impossible to persuade a man to think intellectually when such a situation confronts him as his own child being at the point of death. Accordingly, Jesus used to be severe in his demand for faith as a condition for performing miracles. Without faith, it is impossible to transmit this power. Jesus believed in the omnipotence of faith. He said that all things are possible to him that believeth.

"These signs shall follow them that believe; in my name shall they cast out devils; they shall preach with new tongues; they shall take up serpents; and if they drink any deadly thing, it shall not hurt them; they shall lay hands on the sick, and they shall recover" (Mark 16:17).

Jesus said clearly that miracles are to be expected only in the midst of believers.

(MARK 9:22-23)

85

LOVE IMPLIES A DANGEROUS THOUGHT

I NEVER can forget the time when my soul, besieged by the fear of death and terrors on each hand, learned of Jesus' love and took refuge in the gospel. That is, a simple gospel. It is the good news that death is swallowed up in the victory of love.

How I feared death when I lived in that lonesome province of Awa, where at a burial service the dead were clothed in attire suitable for a journey to the other world. All sorts of horrible portents filled the ceremony, such as the curses of the gods of earth or water and visitations by fires and storms. It was all a terror to me. I even rued that I was born, and wished I had not been.

Then it was that I heard the tidings that God is Love. That was a good report. What could it be but the gospel truth? The man who declared that he forgave sinners was crucified. I saw of a sudden that love is consistent with danger. Yes, indeed, no aspiration is more dangerous than love! Police officers, government authorities, listen! Love is a dangerous motive. Jesus preached love, and he was executed on the Cross!

(I JOHN 2:1-3)

86

THE EXPLOSION OF A SOUL

On account of their love, sinners cease to sin, men of property are deprived of their prestige, the privileged classes lose their status, and authorities in high positions feel themselves in jeopardy. These revolutions are all the burstings of the power that love contains.

But love will remain love despite its dangers! What a contradiction! What irony! But since it is a fact, we can only accept it. Why is love such a peril to every stable order? There is a reason for it. To attend a sick person requires love. To inaugurate a revolution is an exhibition of love! To restore a sinner is love, too! Love runs these risks forever! Whatever shrinks from risk cannot be love. Love means taking a chance. The crisis love produces we call a cross. Love means creating existence where there had been none. Love is what changes darkness into light, sinners into saints, and life on earth into the Heavenly Kingdom. Love possesses this adventurous quality, and whenever it is called into play, it plays an active role. Love is identical with activity. Love is the explosion of a soul!

(MATTHEW 10:35-37)

87

I LIVE; YET NOT I

"I AM crucified with Christ: nevertheless I live; yet not I, but Christ liveth in me." A man who uses such words must have undergone terrible agony to justify them. The burden must have proved too heavy for him, and to have got rid of it he must have given up his life. But he must have reappeared, his body freed of its incubus and his flesh again active with tremendous force. The idea might be expressed by saying Paul made of his body a coffin. It is an awful conception that the coffin was alive as a new body. But if we were to appreciate the religious experience of the first century, we must grasp it at its depth. This saying is a daring one even for Paul, the apostle of Jesus Christ. On what occasion did he utter it? The provocation must have been a series of frustrations and defeats. This conviction was announced by a man who felt in his anguish that the mere fact of his living was a wonder so startling that if it were true, something greater than he was living in him. One who utters such a sentiment is a man who has validly experienced death. His present consciousness is different from his former state. He is like a butterfly emerging from the cocoon which seems to be a dead husk. Henceforth Paul is following Jesus with a coffin on his back.

(GALATIANS 2:20)

88

KNOW THY HEAVENLY FATHER

THERE is an enlightening story that illustrates how we came
to the knowledge of God. An official named Akira Mori
lived at a church in Nakashibuya, Tokyo. His father, Yurei
Mori, was the first minister of education of Japan and a
pioneer in the establishment of the modern educational system. Tragically, however, he was assassinated because of
some misunderstanding.

After this sad event, his family led a lonely life. Akira,
too, passed each day in a sullen dejected mood. One day, at
the Y.M.C.A. Hall he heard a sermon in which he was told
that there is a Father in Heaven. At this news he leaped for
joy, and could not help shedding tears of gratitude on his
way home. He said that his tears loomed like big lights in
the reflection of the twinkling stars when he was passing
around the Double Bridge in front of the Imperial Palace.
By reason of this vision, it is said, he acknowledged himself
a Christian within four days.

I myself had similar experience. My father died when I
was five years old. I suffered keenly because my older
brother led a dissipated life. As I grew a little older, I read
the Sermon on the Mount, and then I clearly discerned that
God is my father, and throwing all else away, I clung to my
Heavenly Creator. God gives us everything when we will
take nothing less than His fatherly comfort.

(LUKE 15:21)

89

TAKE A LITTLE DIFFERENT COURSE

I HAVE learned about Christ through all kinds of books. But I have learned most about him through inscriptions wrought by life itself, through what has been written in the footprints of those who have gone before. A certain missionary was my very first teacher. I learned from this excellent instructor how to love others. Another earnest evangelist taught me much by supporting his family of twelve on a monthly salary of seventeen yen. He was so poor that he had only potatoes to put on his table, but I owe much of my knowledge to his divine compositions. At that time there lived a wayward boy whose name was T. He sported a mustache at the early age of seventeen. And this evangelist, for the purpose of disciplining this boy, shaved off his own mustache and cut his hair. I was appealed to deeply by this example. My Christianity has been transmitted to me from such sources. Mr. Juji Ishii, a noted social worker, also nurtured me. Besides, unlike the ordinary run of religious folks, I took a course in the slums. And I wish my fellow workers would also take such courses of study not listed in the conventional curriculum.

(JOHN 17:18-19)

90

THE LOVE-YOUR-NEIGHBOR
MOVEMENT

THE Love-Your-Neighbor movement need not be opposed by capitalists. The Love-Your-Neighbor movement is not to be implemented by force. All we have to do—we who cherish it—is to proceed as freely and cheerfully as possible. When I was asked by Miss Adams, "Don't you have a report to submit?" I replied, "No, there is no report. Since I'm doing this alone, I owe nobody an accounting."

My Love-Your-Neighbor movement is a little project of my own. A few others who sympathize with its purpose may offer their services voluntarily. Such a large-scale work as Chicago's Hull House is beyond the power and imagination of anyone so poor as I am. Such an organization as Hull House is impossible for everybody, while the small task I have undertaken is, I believe, within the scope of anybody.

If we have money, we should put it to good use as long as it lasts. If we do not have money, we can still aim to do the works of love within our tiny spheres. If we commit ourselves to living in this spirit, our lives will be fruitful. All that is required of us is to help our poor neighbors whosoever they be in our own neighborhoods.

(MATTHEW 22:39-40)

91

MORE THAN VIOLENCE

I STRIVE primarily to be faithful to myself. I cannot compromise with my duty to myself. Therefore, I cannot commit an act of violence against others to oppose violence on their part, knowing that violence is at all times evil. It is terrible to do violence myself for the purpose of correcting it in others. It is self-contradictory to teach that by means of force others are to be restrained from using force. Even though they may be compelled to cease, that is not because they assent from the conviction of their hearts, but only because they are being controlled by a force greater than they could exert.

There may be an occasional case where people repent while they are suppressed. If so, the real motive is their belief in renovation. Force does not convert wrongdoers; only repentance and spiritual growth avail for that. In the individual life, nonresisting love is now generally admitted to be a moral influence. We believe, too, that if there are enough good people it is possible to isolate and educate criminals. If all could have this faith as individuals in the principle of growth and in the power of nonviolent love, such love might be applied to nations. Nations, then, might live with one another on its basis. Force is unnecessary in a truly ideal society, large or small, where even the faults of transgressors may be forgiven.

(ROMANS 12:20)

92

FREEDOM AND EQUALITY THROUGH GROWTH

OUR program of reconstruction must eliminate every compulsion from education. The first care of the teacher is to keep from checking the clear water of love and life springing up within his pupil. Teachers should regard themselves as only the drillers of these artesian wells.

The error of the educators in the past has been that they considered themselves the sources of the water. Instead they are only guardians of the fountains. The way of democracy is not the pursuit of equality, but of growth. Equality truly conceived envisages each generation growing up not only like the one prior to it, but ahead of it as well.

Freedom is an empty idea unless it has this substance. Freedom must be freedom for progress. Nothing is more dangerous than freedom to stay in the same place. Equality through growth, and freedom through growth can be achieved only through the processes of education. Real reconstruction of society can be accomplished only through the operation of education through love.

(MATTHEW 23:9-10)

93

SYMPATHY WITH SINNERS

RATHENAU said, "It is a mistake to attempt to wipe all the rich people out of existence to quicken social reconstruction, for the rest are all poor. The secret of the reconstruction movement must be to make all the poor people rich." The idea of Jesus was along this line, too. Hence, he could advise the wealthy young man sympathetically to elevate the state of his inferiors. Here is exhibited the humanity of Jesus.

Always he abounded in sympathy for sinners. He said that God accepted the prayer of the penitent rather than that of the self-righteous Pharisee. This insight was as far remote from the ideas of the Jews in those days as heaven is remote from earth. Sympathy for humanity must include the victims of sin in its embrace.

Jesus was the most human of men, which is to say he most completely possessed the nature of God. No matter how far the social movement may move forward, when it forfeits this capacity for oceanlike sympathy, its effect is halted. Consequently, it is most necessary that spiritual perceptiveness keep pace with the progress of social reconstruction. Jesus, by nature a friend of the weak and a sympathizer with sinners, was the real fountainhead of the Son-of-God social movement. The social movement, founded on His Messiahship, was a religious movement before it became a social one.

(LUKE 18:13-14)

94

PARTICIPATION BY AFFLICTION

WHEN sorrow, loneliness and anguish afflict us, some supernatural power intervenes. Such rescue is an indispensable
effect of religion. Paul was pulled from the pit by a mysterious happening and became a disciple of Jesus. Originally he
had deemed Jesus' religion to be the worst heresy possible.
But of this error he repented and, reverencing this master
whom he had formerly hated, he traveled everywhere along
the coasts of the Mediterranean Sea to propagate the gospel
of a Cross. Thereafter he was never ashamed of bearing the
Cross of Jesus.

Japan is not only poor as a nation, but is also full of a
multitude of poor people. And what is worse, these people
lack a redeeming faith. Every family has a host of worries,
and every housewife has constant provocation to shed secret
tears. On every such grievous occasion, we should think of
Paul the disciple. He forever looked up at Christ's figure
and was never discomfited by the Cross. Thus we, too, gain
strength to be ashamed of nothing, and both sorrow and
vexation disappear. But the religion of the Cross does not
merely get us out of afflictions of our own but it makes us
willing to help others by sharing their plight. This power,
further, pertains to the essence of the teachings of Jesus.

(PHILIPPIANS 2:17)

CONSOLATION TO A RUINED MAN

JESUS did not merely flaunt a high-sounding ideal. If he had done only that, he would not have differed from the Pharisees, and his message would have been no better than the sayings of Confucius. What transformed Jesus into the Savior was his firm belief in the possibility of healing sick and dying souls by leaping over the barrier which stretched between holiness and sin and by purifying the sinner of his sins. Thus Jesus was nowise ashamed of befriending the basest bribe-taking official. Matthew, the writer of the Gospel, was a tax collector. He was excluded from the patriotic crusade of the Jews, was publicly ostracized by the Pharisees, and despised by the common people as one who belonged to some polluted class. Therefore, he could well appreciate the sympathy and the love of Christ when Christ spoke kindly to him. "He loves a ruined man like me! He forgives the sins of such a sinful man as I!"—this reaction was the beginning of Matthew's redemption. Hence, the Gospel of Matthew stands as the link between Judaism and the Christian principle of the new era, which is one of sympathy with the lost, the depraved and the helpless.

The Gospel of Matthew, bestowing limitless consolation and power to those who are despised and neglected, truly impresses us with the depth of Christ's affection toward the publican who later wrote it.

(MATTHEW 4:24)

96

GAIN OF LEARNING CONTENTMENT

IT is said that the mansion of a certain marquis was so vast that it boasted some three thousand sliding doors, and ten servants were kept to open and to close them every day. But if civilization means efficiency and convenience, to possess such an atrocity must be considered as a troublesome impediment. Unlike this mansion, the house in which I lived at Shinkawa was the climax of convenience. There were alleys both in front of and at the back of my house. At the call "Telegram!" all that I had to do was to put my hand out of my bedroom window, saying, "Give it to me here!" All the year through I never locked the doors of my abode.

When the great earthquake occurred, a policeman was stationed at Eitai-bashi Bridge in Tokyo to warn fugitives who were fleeing with huge bales of property strapped on their backs, "Dangerous! Throw your baggage away! Throw it away!" Nevertheless, some of them did not heed the admonition and insisted on saving their possessions. As a result, they caught fire and were burned to death. Can we not now listen to the advice of this policeman? Of course it is necessary to preserve the wherewithal to live and to eat. But I tell you it is always a good plan to discard useless things and unnecessary encumbrances. Jesus said truly, "What shall it profit a man, if he shall gain the whole world, and lose his own soul?"

(I TIMOTHY 6:6)

97

OUR LORD OF LIGHT!

O GOD, keep the whole land of Japan in Thy protection,
O Lord of our blessings and mercies!
Wipe out sin from this land, lift it up from the depth of
sorrow,
O Lord of our shining light!
Save us from dark grief and misfortune, Lord of all nations!

Tempests choose to take their course here, earthquakes and
tidal waves threaten to overwhelm us,
Our Lord, take care of our country!
Let our country enter into the everlasting victory,
Where no clamor of strife, but the voice of peace and mutual
aid we hear!

Bless this nation with Thy wisdom, O Lord, so that the poor
May not be oppressed and the rich may not be oppressors;
Make this a nation having no ruler except GOOD,
A nation having no authority save that of LOVE.

(ISAIAH 60:20)

98

THE PROLETARIAN AGE

IN olden times men were nomads and roamed about continually. But nowadays the ground on which men stand does the moving. Our structures are built on shifting sand. In the economic system of capitalism people are beset with anxiety concerning the foundation on which they stand, confronting the menace of unemployment or a depression. Nobody knows when he may be ordered to vacate the house he lives in, or when he may be discharged and have to seek for another job. What an insecure and uneasy life!

Nevertheless, even the people who lead this unstable existence, if they cherish the human love Jesus preached, and help and love one another, can get rid of that terror through God's aid and favor. Even proletarians condemned to the status of wage slaves can feel secure through God's power.

The way of the economic lowly must be the way of the eternal Cross. And the master who is ignorant of how to serve is not entitled to employ other men. The future world will be the inheritance of the meek. Each of us must shoulder his cross and help create the new world by means of the sacrifice which no king can imitate. Jesus was the typical common man. He abandoned everything destitute folks are without, and he gained eternal life as rewarding compensation.

(REVELATION 21:4)

99

MEANING OF INCARNATION

INCARNATION means the lifting up of this lower world by a power from a higher One. Herein lies the real significance of the birth of Jesus. Jesus, relinquishing the form of God, took the form of a man.

"Let this mind be in you, which was also in Christ Jesus: Who, being in the form of God, thought it not robbery to be equal with God; but made himself of no reputation, and took upon him the form of a servant, and was made in the likeness of men: And being found in fashion as a man, he humbled himself, and became obedient unto death, even the death of the cross." Realizing this is the real Christmas. Furthermore, the spirit of Christmas supplies the fundamental drive behind the Christian social movement in modern times. He who is appointed to occupy a high position in society, abandons his freedom for self-aggrandizement in order to serve the common people by humbling himself. The laboring classes, too, must consent to give up some of the rights which they might be able to enforce. Right here the fundamental principle of the movement for social betterment can be discerned. Without renunciation, those in heaven remain there forever, and those on earth are destined to stay there permanently. Shattering this barrier between heaven and earth, Christ descended to the manger.

(MARK 9:36)

100

THOSE LOOKING UP TO HEAVEN

WHEN Jesus was born, two visitations were paid to him. The first group of welcomers consisted of shepherds who had witnessed his glory on the hills. They were keeping watch by night over their flocks, and they were the first to see the light. This rule never fails in any age. Laborers and hard-working people understand Christ. They can glimpse the gleam in the midst of the night's toil. There are no woods to conceal the sky. The sole pleasure darkness affords is to look up at the stars. Since the shepherds were reaching in hope, they could see its bursting. Though they belonged to the disinherited, they were upward-looking folk.

The second group that came to Jesus was composed of astronomers. They were students of things above. Herschel said, "Those who cannot discover God through a telescope are fools." Greek religion started from the idea of heaven. Because astrology was introduced to the Greeks by the Persians who were accustomed to observe the heavens, the word "holiness" was introduced to their language. Light must be unobstructed. Learning is that light. If the universe is perceived through it, the existence of God and the advent of salvation will be clearly seen. Even those who do not have the gospel through the Bible will come to understand God through gazing at the stars.

(MATTHEW 2:10)

101

TWO OLD PERSONS

WHEN Jesus was born, those who followed the workers and scholars in their recognition of him were two old persons. Simeon and Anna had been waiting twoscore years with prayers and devotion for Christ to come. All at once a poor carpenter and his wife brought Jesus to the temple bearing as their trifling offering a pair of turtle doves, instead of lambs, to make their sacrifice of thanksgiving. To these two watchers Christmas came forty days later than to the wise men and the shepherds. Yet they discovered the same Son of God who would save the world, in Jesus who might have been mistaken for just another child. That day they found the Messiah was Christmas for them, and it is the same with us today. Paul said, "Let this mind be in you, which was also in Christ Jesus"; Christmas is of no value for us if Christ remains unborn and outside us. Even when we sing, "Joy to the world, the Lord is come . . . ," what does our carol signify if our hearts are empty? The first nativity happened nineteen hundred years ago, but unless his birth is repeated in our hearts today, what difference did it make?

Amid the distress of the world of today, we must arise as sons of God to proclaim the words of life, and to shine brightly as the reflectors of Christ and the embodiments of his power. Herein resides the true meaning of Christmas.

(LUKE 2:23)